CLIMB A LONELY HILL

'A remarkable first novel . . . The possibilities of the situation are exploited to the full, and the relationship is beautifully developed.' *Sunday Times*

'The children are real children, frail and recognizable; one cares about their fate.' *Times Literary Supplement*

'An Ivan-Southall-ish tale of the Outback; just as distinguished and just as good.' *New Statesman*

'The two children's plight and struggle to survive against odds is made really exciting.' *Observer*

Other titles in Lions

DOCKIE *Martin Ballard*
THE MOCK REVOLT *Vera and Bill Cleaver*
GHOSTLY ENCOUNTERS *Susan Dickinson*
GHOSTLY EXPERIENCES *Susan Dickinson*
THE WEIRDSTONE OF BRISINGAMEN *Alan Garner*
THE MOON OF GOMRATH *Alan Garner*
ELIDOR *Alan Garner*
THE OWL SERVICE *Alan Garner*
THE OUTSIDERS *S. E. Hinton*
THAT WAS THEN THIS IS NOW *S. E. Hinton*
MONSTER MUSEUM *Alfred Hitchcock*
SPELLBINDERS IN SUSPENSE *Alfred Hitchcock*
SHUDDERS AND SHAKES *Anne Ingram*
EYE-WITNESS *Alan C. Jenkins*
WHEN HITLER STOLE PINK RABBIT *Judith Kerr*
THE THIRD CLASS GENIE *Robert Leeson*
THE HILL OF THE RED FOX *Allan Campbell McLean*
MASTER OF MORGANA *Allan Campbell McLean*
THE YEAR OF THE STRANGER *Allan Campbell McLean*
THE SHAPE OF THREE *Lilith Norman*
THE MORNING GLORY *Margaret Paice*
THE GUNSHOT GRAND PRIX *Douglas Rutherford*
THE MIN-MIN *Mavis Thorpe Clark*
THE SWORD IN THE STONE *T. H. White*

CLIMB A LONELY HILL

Lilith Norman

COLLINS: LIONS

First published 1970 by William Collins Sons and Co Ltd
14 St James's Place, London, SW1
First published in Lions 1972
Second Impression 1975

Printed in Great Britain
by William Collins Sons and Co Ltd, Glasgow

FOR ARNOR

CHAPTER ONE

Slowly Jack opened his eyes.

His eyelids felt gummy and swollen, and his head ached. All he could see was a great layer of cracked ice. Like party ice, he thought. He closed his eyes again. That's what he needed—ice. Great crystal mounds and mountains of cold ice, clinking and sliding in pyramids all over his body. His body felt strange, too. Stiff and bloated; like it was when he woke up from a sweltering summer night's sleep.

Jack forced his eyes open again, and was suddenly aware of a snuffling, sobbing noise somewhere behind him.

Consciousness flooded over him. Susan. It must be Sue crying! But why was she crying? Where were they?

The car and Uncle Bert! They were travelling with Uncle Bert, and something had happened. An accident? Jack's eyes slowly focused. That wasn't ice at all, it was the windscreen of the car, starred into a craze of white fragments. Gingerly he turned his head, but all he could see was the back of the front seat, and he realized he was half-sitting on the floor. He eased himself carefully up, and peered over the top. His sister was hunched up in a tight ball on the back seat, whimpering softly to herself.

'It's all right, Sue,' he said.

Sue lifted her head and stared at him unbelievingly.

'I thought you were dead,' she sniffed forlornly. Her face was grimy with tear streaks, and her blue eyes looked accusingly at her older brother. There was dried blood under her nose, and smeared amongst the dust and tears. She must have hit her nose an awful wallop when we crashed, thought Jack. He pulled a rather grimy handkerchief from the pocket of his jeans and passed it back to Sue.

'Here, dry your eyes and wipe your face over.'

Sue accepted the hankie, rubbed gingerly at her face, and blew her nose.

'What about Uncle Bert?' she asked, when she had succeeded in spreading the grime more evenly over her face rather than cleaning it.

'Crikey! I forgot all about him,' said Jack guiltily. At least he almost had, he admitted to himself. But all the time he'd been attending to Sue, he had been aware of the still, ominous bulk of his uncle bent over the steering wheel on the seat beside him.

'I think he's dead, too,' said Sue, and the tears trembled in her voice.

'Oh, come off it,' he laughed, in an attempt to cheer her up. 'You said that about me, and I'm okay. He's probably just stunned. After all, we must've come an awful crash, because you got a bloody nose and I was knocked out.'

Despite his optimism, Jack knew there was no avoiding it any longer. He'd have to find out if, and how badly, Uncle Bert was hurt, and do something about it. But a sixth sense made him uneasy.

'Look, Sue, while I'm fixing Bert up, you get out and wash your face—it looks terrible. Use a bit of water from one of the drums in the back.'

'Okay. But my nose hurts.'

'Well, just dab it gently, silly. Go on, out you get.'

Sue uncurled fully, and leaned over to open the door.

'I can't get out. It won't open.'

'Oh, for heaven's sake! You know that side's always stuck. Use the right hand door.'

Sue bounced across the seat and pushed the handle down. The door opened with ease, and she slipped out and stood there for a few minutes, her eyes fixed on Uncle Bert.

'Gee, he looks terrible, Jack.'

'All right, all right! He'll be okay in a minute. Just go and wash your face.' Jack's fear made him speak more roughly than he meant to, but Sue's bedraggled little figure in its cheap faded cotton shift, the too-thin brown legs, and the feet thrust into worn thongs, made him regret his harshness.

'Go on, Sue,' he repeated, more gently, 'we'll be fine.'

Sue trailed obediently round to the back of the car, but Jack heard her mutter, 'Gee you're bossy' as she disappeared from sight.

He turned back, and stared for a minute at the frosty windscreen. If his uncle was badly hurt, he didn't know what he'd do. In all his fourteen years he had coped with many problems, both physical and emotional, by the one simple method—running away. He didn't run away physically, but he ran away inside himself, by acting the fool and pretending that nothing mattered. Jack never stopped to question his behaviour. All he knew was that it worked. And when you're the son of the town drunk, that is all that counts.

Jack put out his hand and touched his uncle's arm. The skin still felt warm and alive, and Jack drew a sigh of relief.

'Uncle Bert! Uncle Bert!'

He shook his uncle gently, then more firmly, and a hum of black bush flies whirred into the air and settled again immediately. How did you tell how badly hurt someone was? Jack wondered. He felt for the wrist, where the arm hung limply down beside the gear lever. Carefully he pressed his fingers around the red, sunburnt skin, trying first one position and then another. Sometimes he thought he could perceive a faint pulse beat, but the more he concentrated, the more uncertain he became. Frustrated, he rested the hand on the seat beside him, where it lay relaxed but oddly unnatural-looking, the sun glinting on the strong golden hairs and the heavily calloused palm and fingers grimed with deep cracks from which no amount of soap and water could remove the ground-in oil and earth. The massive, capable hand suddenly seemed pathetic and defenceless.

Even as he watched a couple of flies settled on the still thumb and walked purposefully across the bent knuckle. A third fly lit on the back of the hand and turned carefully around, seeming to avoid, as if by design, the large yellow-brown blotched freckles.

'Damn these blasted flies,' swore Jack to himself. With an angry wave he shooed them off his uncle's bent head and the back of his neck.

'I'll have to get him out and lie him down,' he thought. Gently he started to ease his uncle's head back against the seat. It was then that he saw it. The reddish-black stain spreading around the wound where the shattered steering column, like a stake, had slid cleanly and quickly through a life.

A cold sweat of nausea flooded over Jack, the shattered windscreen glistened into a blur of white snow, and he was only vaguely conscious of fumbling the door open and staggering out on to the earth, where he vomited in great retching spasms. At last the heaving lessened and he was able, by gulping hard, to control his spastic stomach muscles. Completely exhausted he sank to the ground, feeling only relief as the burning air dried the damp sweat on his body and brought a comforting warmth to the coldness that seemed to chill him into immobility.

'Jack! Jack!' Sue's shrill cries penetrated unwillingly.

'Jack!' Now she was kneeling beside him and shaking him. 'Jack! What's the matter?'

Wearily Jack forced his eyes open. Sue was staring at him with alarm. He tried to concentrate, but his mind kept sheering away to something horrible in the car. Think . . . think . . . look at Sue. Concentrate on her. She looked better now that she had washed her face. Her nose was a bit wobbly, either from the bump it had had, or from all that crying.

'I'm all right now, Sue. It was just shock, I guess—and Uncle Bert.'

'What about Uncle Bert? Can I help him?' Sue started to get to her feet.

'*No!*' His voice was sharp with panic. 'No! He's okay. No, no he's not really.' He'd have to tell her. 'He's . . .

he's dead, I think. You can't do anything for him. Stay here.'

Sue subsided on to the soil again beside Jack, her eyes searching his in an effort to comprehend.

Jack spoke quickly, 'I don't think it hurt him. It must have been awfully quick. But I don't want you to go back there, Sue.'

Suddenly he felt a compulsion to think about it, to touch and probe it—the fact of death. To try and grapple with this mystery of the spark that one minute was there and the next was gone, silently, like the exhalation of a breath. What was it that had gone, and that left his uncle's body so much less than his uncle had been?

Jack had never seen a dead person before. He'd seen plenty of death, of course. Dead sheep, dead crows, wedge-tail eagles crucified on fences, goannas and rabbits squashed on the road, roos struck by cars, and bundles of pink and grey feathers that had once been galahs, quivering into mimic life as cars swooped by. His mother had died, too, but that had been in the hospital, 150 miles away. It was only something he was *told* about, a sudden shock and then a gradually absorbed sense of loss, for at the age of eight he had not been able to put a personal vision on death. It had been a word and an absence—not a grim physical reality like Uncle Bert's.

Uncle Bert, his father's brother, was a happy gregarious man, who yet spent much of his life alone. An itinerant mechanic, as witness the car beside them: a four-seater Land-Rover-type chassis covered in at the back like a utility, with roughly hand-beaten and hand-painted panel work. In this monstrosity, which he vowed would give any city driver a fit of the Joe Blakes, Uncle Bert had covered thousands of miles of New South Wales, from the Murray River up to The Corner, and across to the black soil plains of Moree. Building a spider's web of criss-crossing journeys. Uncle Bert travelled to wherever there was the likelihood of casual work, or a bit of gold panning, or some opal gouging, or fencing. Anywhere, in fact, where his home-made van could go, and that was most places; any job, as long as it didn't involve riding a horse.

Uncle Bert was, or had been, unique amongst bushmen in that he not only refused to ride a horse—he couldn't ride.

'Horses,' he used to snort, hitching his trousers which hung precariously and miraculously on his hips below the bulge of his stomach. 'They only shake the guts out of a man. And when you've got a gut like mine, you want to look after it. Horses,' he'd continue, getting on to his favourite subject, 'they ruined me brother. Your dad, that is. All that horsebreaking when he was young. Shook his liver to bits and addled his brain. Not but what I don't reckon he carried it a bit too far. Dan Clarke used to be the best stockman around when he was a kid. Even until he took that fall, in fact. Never reckoned he'd live after that. Even when he came out of hospital I c'n remember him nearly crying with the pain in his legs. That's when he really started drinking. Reckoned the booze killed the pain. I don't blame him. After all, he's me own brother, but I reckon when a bloke's got a family he ought to pull in his horns a bit. Still, I'm not married—haven't got any kids either, not that I know of.' Here Bert would bellow with laughter, and Jack and Sue would grin shyly. 'So maybe you kids can have two sorts of dads. Between us perhaps we'll make one decent one.'

Guiltily, Jack half-wished that Uncle Bert were really his father. It wasn't that he hated his father, for Dad wasn't a cruel man, but Jack hated what he was and did. He hated the ineffectual promises and the treats that never materialized; the shambling, slurring figure stumbling through the streets, or crumpled in a shop doorway, or snoring on the floor at home. He hated the reek of beer and cheap wine, the unshaven face, the vacant unfocused gaze, and the mumbling, drunken, meaningless love: 'That's my Jack . . . best son . . . man ever had . . . goo' boy' when he helped his father to stagger home. He hated the shame he felt as his father begged for drinking money, and the way other men shoved him aside without even bothering to look at him. They did it as thoughtlessly and carelessly as they'd push away a fawning dog with their boot. He hated being the butt of the teachers' gibes at school because he seldom had a chance to keep his work up-to-date. He hated the way the other kids would trail along mimicking his father lurching from side to side. Only they didn't do that so often now, for Jack could do an even better imitation of a drunk than any of them. He did it for laughs, and it didn't seem to hurt so much then.

It was a sense of responsibility to his brother Dan's children that had made Bert detour several hundred miles out of his way to pick Jack and Sue up during the Christmas holidays.

'Heard of an almost forgotten diggings out off the old Weilgumpie turn-off, and thought I'd try me luck for a week or so in the New Year. How about you kids coming along?'

Bert had arrived on Boxing Day, and Dan Clarke had readily given his permission. With the self-reproaches and easy tears of the partly sober, Dan recalled the sparse and drunken Christmas Day, a day on which he had promised faithfully to stay sober, but which he had mainly spent sprawled stuporously on the rickety camp stretcher on the back verandah. Although they had learned to expect it, Jack and Sue had felt sick with disappointment.

For months they had carefully put aside whatever they could spare from their meagre funds. Dad's pension and the Child Endowment didn't amount to much, and Jack earned some more with his paper delivery morning and evening. and occasional odd jobs at week-ends. There was enough to buy food of the cheapest sort, but the money rarely ran to kerosene for the lamps, their weatherboard shack down near the river not being connected to the electricity supply. Although Dad never failed to give them a few dollars when he cashed the welfare cheques, it didn't run to extras. At Sue's insistence, Jack kept this housekeeping money in an old tin. The tin had a number of hiding places, the latest being under the rubbish heap behind the lavatory. If it hadn't been carefully hidden, Dad would have found it and drunk the lot.

With the money they had saved, they celebrated Christmas. Together they bought a couple of handkerchiefs and a packet of razor blades for Dad. From his own earnings, Jack purchased two new exercise books, which he laboriously covered with spare pieces of wallpaper discarded by the hardware store where Jack occasionally worked as delivery boy, while Sue's present to her brother was a new ballpoint pen for school. The rest of their savings went on some slices of tinned ham, a small tinned Christmas pudding, and a sprig of plastic holly.

They ate their festive meal to the accompaniment of Dad's mumbling and snores.

When Uncle Bert arrived, a conscious-stricken Dan Clarke had been staring sombrely at his two gifts. He'd given them nothing in return; at least he could let them go for a holiday.

'You're a real mate, Bert. They're good kids. You take them off and give 'em a break and a bit of fun.'

So Jack hurriedly arranged for Mick Lindsay to take over his paper run until he returned, and he and Sue helped Uncle Bert make preparations. Bert had loaded the car up with an extra drum of petrol, two spare drums of water, and a few tins of food.

'Don't want too much of that rubbishy tinned muck. Just some flour and sultanas for a damper. Apart from that, we'll live off the country. Shoot a young roo and have all the fresh meat we need,' chuckled Bert, as he put his rifle (scrounged from the Army during the war), and a box of cartridges in the back.

Sue's battered old school suitcase held all the two children's needs, not that they had much to pack anyway. A change of underwear, a toothbrush each, and a pair of faded shorts and blouse for Sue, on the grounds that they would be more practical to wear once they made permanent camp. Shorts, however, were too uncomfortable in the car, where the sun could burn your legs raw in a day's driving, and turn the leather of the seats into a sizzling hot-plate that made you leap with anguish as your flesh touched it. Jack took even less clothing—just the jeans and shirt he was wearing, and his old desert boots. He hoped to be doing a man's share of the work with Uncle Bert, and boots at least had the virtue of keeping out the hot sand and most of the more persistent insects. Uncle Bert had said there was supposed to be a small waterhole near the diggings, so perhaps, Jack thought, they might even be able to go swimming. Still, underpants would do for that. In fact, underpants were more effective than his old red trunks which, as well as having stretched alarmingly, had developed a number of almost indecent holes.

Thus meagrely equipped, and content to rely largely on Uncle Bert's skill as a bushman, the three had set out.

CHAPTER TWO

They left Karkarook on the Monday morning. Uncle Bert had picked them up just after eight, and they had all gone down to the Coronation Café and Milk Bar for breakfast. The Coronation was the only café in town, and Con Constantinos, the Greek proprietor, stayed open while there was the slightest chance of a customer to be served. Everyone patronized the Coronation. Schoolchildren bought handfuls of lollies or iceblocks, drank their milkshakes and ice cream sodas, or downed banana splits while playing the juke box. Housewives dropped in for a cup of tea and sandwiches, and stayed to gossip, convincing themselves that the two huge fans, rotating trance-like from the fly-spotted ceiling, gave the café a coolness that the furnace-fire main street lacked. Shearers, sheep farmers, the occasional travelling salesman, all looked upon the Coronation as their headquarters.

Here, at a table in imitation red marble laminex, the three had eaten enormously of steak and eggs, liberally slathered with sauce, toast, and pots of tea.

'A bloke needs an extra good breakfast when he's starting out,' Uncle Bert had proclaimed, and Jack and Sue were only too ready to agree with him. During the meal, Con and Uncle Bert had chatted, in a casual fashion, about the weather, always of prime importance in the west, and the forthcoming trip.

'I heard the road out to Weilgumpie's pretty bad,' said Con, when he learned where they were heading. 'They had the grader out there just before the last big rains, and then the trucks come out and churn it up terrible.'

'Yeah? Well, I reckon me old van can get through most places. Might be a bit rough, but at least she'll have dried out now. Not that we expect any trouble,' added Uncle

Bert, 'but if the old car does jack up on me, it's just a matter of making camp beside her and waiting. Someone's bound to come along some day, and we've got plenty of water. Enough for a couple of weeks, and we could hold out longer, unless these two runts decide to bathe in it.' He reached across and tousled Jack's hair affectionately. 'Anyway, they reckon there's permanent water in some of them rock basins near the diggings. We'll be right.'

'No fear of that,' agreed Con, 'and I hope you find plenty gold.'

'If we do, I'll bring you back a nugget for young Nick, as big as his head.'

'You better hurry, well, he's growing every day. Soon he bigger than his old man.' Con smiled proudly. His six-year-old son was living proof of Con's faith in his new country. Yet while Con laughed and talked and joked with Bert Clarke, his mind struggled to understand this man who seemed content to chase after crazy, wild goose gold mines; who had a broken-down old car, and probably a hundred dollars in the bank if he was lucky. He, Con Constantinos, had several thousand dollars carefully saved, and this money would be an even more respectable sum by the time his son, Nick, was grown up. Enough to start him in a small business, or even send him to university, if that was what he wanted.

In the end Con decided that, while he liked Bert personally, he also despised him for being weak. What Con couldn't understand was that a disinclination to slave for ten or twelve or fourteen hours a day was not synonymous with lack of character. Con came from a land of heart-breaking toil, with few rewards, and this had given him a drive to acquire material security which was absent from the heavy, casual Australian sitting at his table. Yet both were kind, good men. They were just different.

Breakfast finished, the three piled into Uncle Bert's utility and headed north-west. Karkarook soon vanished behind them; only its name remained, echoed in the desolate call of the crows which cawed endlessly overhead.

The makeshift body of the old car creaked and groaned as it clumped and bottomed over ruts and potholes. The country was always the same and yet, somehow, never monotonous. Scattered tufts of saltbush grew in varying shades of grey from blue through to silver, toning down the hard redness of the soil. And always behind them a cloud of talcum-fine bulldust hung in a two-mile trail, so that the ute resembled a rackety, earthbound comet.

At first the country was uniformly flat, with stunted gums, mulga, and an occasional leopard wood tree with its striking black-and-white blotched bark. Other cars were rare, but every few miles they would pass signs that the country was still inhabited. Sometimes the sign was merely a post pointing down a barely definable dirt track to some unidentifiable station a mile or two off the road. More often it was a roadside mailbox, ranging from a broken wooden box to a carefuly painted and lettered 44-gallon drum. The drums served not only for mail, but also for bread, stores and general deliveries. The station names painted on them reflected the whims of the owners, from a staunch loyalty to the Britain that originally bred them, to pure Australian, and everything in between. There was Thirlmere, Mirrabooka, Upson Downs (a bad pun), Arabella, Pitjicarribee, Kirrloo Kirrloo, Loch Linnhe, Just in Time, The Homestead, Wantabadgery, and many more.

The travellers stopped for lunch at Ghill, a township consisting of one general-store-and-post-office, and a few shabby cottages standing forlornly in weed-filled yards. At the store they bought sandwiches—real doorstoppers and rather stale, but exceedingly filling. These they washed down with tepid soft drinks, since the store's refrigerator was fighting a losing battle against the intense heat.

After Ghill, the signs of settlement grew farther and farther apart. It was now often fifteen or twenty miles between each mailbox or station turning, and the stations themselves were frequently a dozen or more miles back from the road. This was the country of loneliness, where a sheep station was a tiny self-contained settlement of its own; where a trip to even such an unimpressive town as Karkarook was an infrequent event, since it involved nearly a day's drive, and an overnight stay at the Spartan, high-ceilinged hotel. The sparse vegetation in the paddocks might only support one sheep to every twenty acres or so, and the properties had to be correspondingly large in order to carry several thousand sheep. This added to the isolation. It was the world of the wireless transceiver, through which was received news, school lessons, medical advice and care, gossip, and most other outside human contact.

Unnoticed, the ute jolted past these invisible station worlds.

By the first night they had reached a bridge spanning one of the tributaries of the Darling. Like most of the waterways, it was no longer flowing, but there were a number of deep waterholes on each side of the bridge. Uncle Bert swung the car off to the right, and they bumped and clattered along a barely discernible depression, which could have been a seldom-used track, or merely a stormwater washaway. It was hard to tell.

Carefully dodging tree roots and hummocks as best he could, Uncle Bert jounced along the bank until a slight curve hid them from the road. Here the bank stood some twenty feet above the level of the water. There was little scrub and no grass, just massive gums, gnarled and tangled and twisted, their giant roots grabbing the soil like huge, straining knuckles. On the opposite bank similar trees loomed, and Jack could see that half their roots were hanging bare against the exposed cutting where flood waters had churned and swirled the soil away.

Bert parked under a magnificent gum, gunned the motor briefly, and then let it die away with a cough and a kick as he switched off the ignition. A flock of pink and grey galahs flew off protesting, and settled farther up the bank squabbling disgruntledly. Bert heaved himself out of the car, stretched, and then, pulling out his battered tobacco tin, lovingly rolled himself a cigarette. The scent of burning tobacco brought an alien aroma to the bush, the first sign that man, and with him civilization, had intruded.

Bert was a big man, just on six feet tall, and solid framed. What had once been nearly sixteen stone of hard muscle was now beginning to soften to fat. His hair was fair with a slight gingery tinge, whereas Jack and Sue had inherited their father's almost black hair. His skin, which in an English climate would have been fair and soft, had been coarsened and reddened by the perpetual Australian sunshine to a burned brick red, mottled with large freckles. His thick twill trousers were stained and wrinkled from rain and sweat, and his short-sleeved shirt was undone to the waist, revealing a dilapidated singlet. On his sockless feet he wore great clumping boots which laced up well over the ankle, and had soles that looked too thick ever to bend. They were ex-Army disposals issue, and had probably not seen a coat of polish since the day he had bought them. Dried mud, months old, clung to the heels, and the uppers, especially the toes, were scuffed and torn from taking exploratory kicks at likely-looking rocks.

Having finished his cigarette, Bert stirred into action.

'Righto kids, clear a good space for a fire, and we'll get a meal going before it's too dark.'

Jack and Sue set to, carefully clearing a wide circle of all dead leaves and twigs, until only the bare soil remained. Then they collected a pile of dead wood for the fire. Uncle Bert, meanwhile, had selected a couple of decent-sized stones, scraped a small depression, filled the billy from one of the water drums, and set it on the stones. With a few deft movements he set and lit the fire. To an observer he might have seemed lackadaisical, even lazy. But he had lived long in a climate where conserving energy in the searing heat had become second nature. His movements, like his speech, were slow and considered, but, in fact, every action had been honed down until all irrelevant and unnecessary motion was removed. All that remained were the few basic movements sufficient to complete any task in the shortest and most efficient way.

Once the fire was burning well, Bert unloaded the essentials from the back of his van. Tossing a bundle of sausages to Jack, he said,

'Snags for tea tonight. You and Sue get them started.' He handed Sue the heavy cast-iron frying pan, and its weight was so unexpected she nearly dropped it.

'Careful there, lass.'

Sue grinned back at him, and staggered over to the fire where she plumped the pan down in the sand. A few thick hunks of bread were cut and fried after the sausages were cooked, and a handful of tea was flung into the boiling billy. Uncle Bert liked his tea black, strong and stewed, so thick that, as he said, 'You can stand the spoon up in it.'

'Have you got any milk?' asked Jack.

'Milk? What a bunch of sissies!' roared Uncle Bert, disturbing once again the almost settled galahs. Then he winked at them. 'Yeah, I was only joking. Have a rake around in that carton on the left. There's powdered and condensed.'

After a brief search, Jack returned with the tin of powdered milk, prised the lid off, and messily tore back the foil seal. He spooned a heap of milk into his and Sue's mugs, and stirred it around. The tea rapidly turned a deep tan, with undissolved lumps of powdered milk floating around the top. It looked pretty revolting, but with the addition of several generous spoonfuls of sugar it tasted surprisingly good.

Satisfied and content, they sat back.

Uncle Bert collected up the tin plates, the chipped enamel mugs, and the knives and forks.

'I'll do the washing-up tonight,' he said, 'but after that it can be Sue's job, seeing she's the only woman here.' He winked at Jack.

Picking up the cutlery, he plunged each piece up and down into the ground beside him. Then he rubbed several handfuls of earth over the plates, scouring them clean.

'Better than all your detergents,' he chuckled, giving

them a final wipe on his trousers. The mugs he rinsed out with the dregs of the tea, swirling them around and around and then emptying them on to the dying fire. The fire hissed, and spat up little clouds of steam and ash. Methodically Uncle Bert kicked dirt over the remnants, and stamped it down until not even a hurricane could have unearthed it and fanned it into life again.

'Now,' he said, heaving himself to his feet, 'how about a lesson in how to pan for gold, while we've still got a bit of light left.'

Bert collected his battered and rusty old tin dish, and the three of them headed down to the river.

'Of course, you won't find any gold here, or else I'll eat my hat if you do. But I'll show you the sort of places you'd look if you were after alluvial gold.'

'What's that?' asked Sue, who had always thought gold was just gold.

'It's the same as any other, only it's not dug out of mines. Alluvial's washed down by rain and rivers, and it might be miles and miles away from its original reef.

'Now,' continued Uncle Bert, as they reached the water, 'gold's very heavy, so if anything cuts the water flow, gold's the first to drop to the bottom. See, you've got the river coming along like this.' He moved his right hand at a steady pace from right to left in front of him. 'Then you get a rock, or maybe a bend in the river, or a snag.' He doubled his left hand into a huge fist. 'The water comes along and hits it.' Here he brought his right hand slapping up against his left fist. 'The water slows down, and out falls the gold. So you look first near rocks and snags and bends. 'Course, it isn't quite as simple as that, or I'd be living in the lap of luxury meself, but that's the general idea.'

Jack and Sue laughed.

'Now,' Bert went on, 'you've found a likely place, so you get to work.'

He squatted down on his haunches, and tossed generous handfuls of dirt into the pan.

'You pick out all the big stones and chuck 'em away—unless they're nuggets, of course—and then you start.'

He picked up the dish, slopped water into it, and started swirling the water around with a steady motion. Hardly breaking his rhythm he drained the discarded mud away, or added more water, occasionally easing the dregs over with one huge thumb.

'This rim here,' he indicated a ridge running around the dish, 'is to catch the gold in. If you do it right, and you've picked the right spot, you'll find quite a few specks there when you've emptied the dish.

A few more sluicings, and Bert stood up.

'There you are,' he said, 'there's your gold.'

'Where? Let me see!' Sue hopped up and down excitedly.

'No, I was only kidding you, Sue. Those are just bits of gravel.'

'That bit's yellow,' said Jack, pointing to a speck barely the size of a pin's head.

'Where?' Uncle Bert peered closer at the dish. 'By crikey, you're right. You've got keen young eyes all right. Well, you can keep it as your first nugget.'

Jack proudly picked the tiny grain up on the tip of his finger, then tied it in a big knot in the corner of his handkerchief.

Sue was jumping about in anticipation.

'Are we going to stay here, Uncle Bert? Are we? Is this where we'll find gold?'

Uncle Bert grinned at her eagerness. They're good kids, he thought. Poor little Bs, they've never had a chance.

'No, Sue. The place I've got in mind I'm sure about. I reckon this was just a fluke. Of course, you can find a bit of colour almost anywhere hereabouts, but nothing worth working always. Do you know, you can even find gold in the streets?'

'In the streets? Like when the streets of London were paved with gold? Where?' The two flung their questions breathlessly.

'Well, I dunno about the streets of London, but here it's

the streets of Tibooburra. I've heard of blokes panning the gutters and run-offs after rain and finding quite a few ounces over the years.'

'You're kidding,' said Jack.

'Are you calling me a liar, boy?' Uncle Bert frowned ferociously, and, reaching one huge, dripping paw, clamped the back of Jack's neck.

'Oh, no . . .' Jack started to stammer, then he caught the twinkle in his uncle's eye, and started to laugh. 'Go on, Uncle Bert, pull the other leg, it whistles.'

'No, it's a fact, Jack. 'Course, I haven't actually seen it with me own eyes. It only rains there once in a blue moon, but a mate of mine has nine ounces of gold he swears he picked up off the streets.'

Jack and Sue stared at him, half amused and half believing.

'Come on, Jack. Let's see how you go with the dish. Might as well get your hand in.'

Uncle Bert chucked some more dirt in the pan, and handed it to Jack.

'Gosh, it's heavy.'

'Yeah. And it's even heavier with water in it.'

Carefully Jack dipped the pan in the river and started to swirl the dish, his eyes concentrating on the circular motion of the water, and his muscles tense and straining to keep his movements steady and even. It had looked so simple and effortless, but it was not, obviously, as easy as it looked.

'That's not bad,' commented Uncle Bert approvingly. 'It'll come to you with practice. It's just a knack like everything else. Ever tried to pat your head with one hand and rub your stomach with the other? Seems impossible at first, then all of a sudden it comes to you. Then you try swapping hands and actions, and you find you're right back where you started.'

Sue immediately started to follow Uncle Bert's instructions, and doubled up with laughter. Jack swung his head around to watch her, and lost control of his dish, with the result that most of the wash-dirt slopped over into the water.

'Gee, I don't see how you'd ever get anywhere much with that,' he said despondently. 'It'd take a fellow a day to do one dishful.'

'Don't you believe it, Jack. A good man can do, oh, about ten an hour, I reckon.'

'Ten an hour! Gosh, I'd *never* be able to do that.'

'Yes you will. By the end of the week you'll have had so much practice you'll be whizzing through them like a hairy goat.'

Sue, who had given up trying to massage or pummel various bits of her anatomy, and had now recovered her breath, interrupted.

'Let me have a go.'

'Go on,' laughed Jack, 'you wouldn't even be able to lift the dish.'

'I would too!'

'Huh! Like fun.'

'Okay, Jack,' their uncle chipped in, 'give Sue a go.'

Jack handed over the dish, which still contained about two pints of very watery mud—or very muddy water.

Sue crouched down and gave the dish a violent swirl. Her hands slipped on the muddy edge, the water shot towards her, and the whole lot sloshed into her lap.

'I told you so,' crowed Jack, 'now look what you've done.'

'Now then, you two,' threatened Bert, who could see that the familiar brother and sister bantering was going to degenerate into a quarrel, or, worse still from his point of view, tears. 'Just cut that out. There's no harm done. Just swish your frock about in the river and she'll dry clean as a bone by morning. In fact we could all do with a bit of a cooling off, it's still so stinking hot. Jack, buzz up to the ute and find a couple of towels and bring them down.'

Jack shot up the bank, and returned in record time with two grey, torn towels. Both he and Sue loved swimming, but could rarely afford to use the town baths. The three of them stripped down to their underwear, and stepped cautiously into the squelchy mud.

'Just keep near the bank here, and watch out for snags, and no fooling around.'

The twilight was beginning to close in, and the sun was a scarlet globe burning against the black silhouettes of the tree trunks. Sue quickly rinsed her frock, and hooked it over a dead branch where she could collect it on their way back to the camp. They splashed happily about for a few minutes, until Jack discovered that the river held a fascinating supply of leeches. Soon he was pounding along the bank after Sue, who ran screaming away: she hated the horrible slimy things. They ran, and slid, and swam, and played, with a careless freedom they had rarely known.

Gradually the shadows lengthened, until it was difficult to see the outline of the trees on the other side of the river. Finally Uncle Bert called them to order, and after a brisk rub down with the towels they headed back up to the car. Uncle Bert got fully dressed again, except for his boots, but the two children decided to sleep in their underwear, and soon all three were wrapped in their individual blankets. Bert had offered the back of the ute to Sue, but nothing would make her forgo the thrill of sleeping outside.

Although they had spent all their lives in Karkarook, neither of them had ever been right out in the bush, and they had never before slept in the open, under the crisply golden stars and the black velvet night sky.

It was an experience to be savoured and cherished.

CHAPTER THREE

Although Sue was tired after the long day's jolting ride and the horseplay down by the river, she lay awake for a long time. There were so many strangenesses to wonder about.

It was funny how the earth, which had such a layer of dust on it, should be so hard. She wriggled and squirmed, trying to avoid the lumps and tussocks, until eventually she had scooped out a slightly smoother depression which just fitted the curve of her body. Uncle Bert had told her to dig a little hole for her hip bone, but as she always slept on her back, or flat on her tummy, she hadn't bothered. Why should hard rocks and soil turn into the softest dust? she wondered. Mr Yates at school said it was the wind and rain wearing them away, but that didn't seem possible, even over millions of years. How incredible was a million years! Fifty years was such a very long time—Dad was only forty-seven and he was terribly old, and Uncle Bert was even older. One hundred years could just be imagined: it was not quite ten times as old as she was. But anything else was forever, and you couldn't really understand forever.

The stars were millions and millions of miles away, too, yet there they hung like polished gold, and most of them no bigger than that tiny speck Jack had tied in his handkerchief. Yet she, Sue Clarke, lying here on her back, could see them. How could you see for millions of miles? There were so many impossible things happening that you just couldn't believe, even though they were true.

Like this holiday.

She'd never *been* on a holiday before. Of course, she'd *had* all the school holidays, but somehow going away made it a proper holiday for the first time. Until now there'd been nowhere to go, and no one to take them. Mum's mother and father lived somewhere down in Sydney, but they never wrote. Sue had asked Dad about them once, but he'd only got furious.

'Stuck up lot! They always said your mum married beneath herself when she took up with me, but her father was only a tinpot clerk. What's so high and mighty about that? He wouldn't know the back end of a horse from Bondi Beach. Good riddance to the lot of them. Who needs them?'

'I need them,' Sue had thought wistfully. It would have been nice to have gone to Sydney for a holiday, and grandparents were fun: always giving you presents and treats, and spoiling you. Most of the other kids in Karkarook went away at least once or twice a year—to relatives, or to a holiday flat, or caravanning.

Dad's side of the family was even worse. There was only Uncle Bert, and a married sister who lived in America. *She* wrote occasionally, but she might as well live on the moon. Still, Uncle Bert had come good now. Sue wriggled herself into a more comfortable position, and sighed happily.

She listened to the trees creaking and whispering their leaves together in the slight stirring of air. A few frogs glunked down in the river, and some sort of bird cried mournfully. There were faint scufflings and scuttlings on the ground as little nocturnal creatures disturbed the dry leaves and twigs. But they were friendly noises, not scary ones. Even those cold golden stars, winking at her from millions of miles away, were friendly.

She could hear Jack's regular quiet breathing, and Uncle Bert's slight snore. Sue smiled to herself, and twisted happily on to her stomach, her cheek cushioned on one outflung arm. It's going to be beaut, she thought, a holiday to remember for always and always.

And fell asleep.

Jack was the first to wake up the next morning. It was still piccaninny dawn, and the sun was not yet up, though the green light in the east and one high sliver of rosy cloud showed that it was not far off. Birds screamed and chattered and fought raucously in flocks and in pairs. A kookaburra, far off, started a slow chuck, chuck, chuck, which swelled into a flooding cascading crescendo of pealing and chortling that washed over Jack like a physical wave of good humour.

He lifted his head and saw Sue lying sprawled in her twisted heap of blanket. She was still sound asleep. He didn't need to turn his head to Uncle Bert, for he could *hear* he was still sleeping. Quickly Jack unrolled himself from his blanket and stood up. The evening breeze had dropped entirely, and there was already a sense of coming heat. Today was going to be a real scorcher, even worse than yesterday. The river, thought Jack with pleasure, already feeling the silky water soaking the sleep out of his body, and giving him a reservoir of coolness to carry him through the day.

Picking his way through the scattered gear of their camp, he ran lightly down the bank. He was half-way down when a sudden silence shocked him into stillness as though every living creature had disappeared simultaneously from the world. At first he thought it was his own movements which had frightened the birds, but as he remained immobile, and still they were quiet, he knew this was not the reason. For several minutes he stood where he was, listening, straining, part of that tense expectancy. While he did, the first small curve of the sun poked up over the horizon. Still he stood, and the sun grew bigger and bigger. Suddenly, as suddenly as they had ceased, the bush sounds sprang into life again.

Despite himself, Jack was awed. It was as though all the birds had simultaneously become aware that the sun had not yet risen. Perhaps it never would. In consternation they stopped . . . held their breath . . . waited . . . There it came. Yes, yes. More and more. The sun *was* rising again. The world they knew would flourish for one more day. In an outburst of rejoicing, the birds burst into song again.

Thoughtfully Jack continued down for his interrupted swim.

How did birds know just when the sun was coming? Why did they sing like mad before and after, but not *during* those few first minutes of sunrise? Were birds aware of day, and night, and time? He remembered the old dog they once had. It was while Mum was still alive and Nigger, that was his name, turned up at school every afternoon just in time to meet him and go home with him. And ants: they knew when rain was coming, for they ran about more crazily than ever, collecting food and mounding up the entrances to their nests. Or like Dad's legs, which always started to ache before a change in the weather.

Still pondering, Jack plunged into the water and floated lazily on his back, revelling in a new sense of freedom. His life had been pretty free anyway, especially during the last couple of years. Even before then he and Sue had done very much as they pleased, and had brought themselves up, despite the various women Dad had brought home to look after them. Some busybodies had disapproved, he knew. He'd overheard the more righteous citizens mutter 'Disgraceful the way those Clarke children are allowed to run wild,' and similar remarks. But Karkarook was an apathetic little town, and no one had seemed to care sufficiently to report them to the authorities. But freedom in Karkarook hadn't been the same as this. Was 'running wild' different from 'freedom'? Was that it?

He wondered if Sue felt different, too. Although they had a rough-and-ready affection, it rarely revealed itself in words, and Jack realized that he knew very little about his sister's thoughts. Despite the fact that they were flung together by circumstances and isolated by social disapproval, they were both solitary children, and spent much of their time alone, Sue pottering along the river bank, and Jack hanging around the town in search of an audience to admire his capers and tomfoolery. Yet even while he acted the goat, even in a crowd, Jack had been alone . . . lonely.

Now there was no more audience but, strangely, he was no longer lonely. Uncle Bert and Sue—gosh!

The curious and unaccustomed mood of introspection was broken. With a start, Jack realized he had been day-dreaming for longer than he thought, for the sun was now fully up. Kicking and splashing, he swam back to the bank, shook the water out of his hair and eyes, and scrambled up to the camp. He had forgotten to take his towel down with him, but it hardly mattered, for he was nearly dry by the time he came in sight of the others. Already the heat of the sun was burning into his skin, and the coolness of the river was a feeling that his body could scarcely remember.

Uncle Bert and Sue were busy around the fire, and Jack could see that breakfast was almost ready. Slipping round to the front of the ute, he pulled off his damp underpants and spread them on the bonnet to dry. Hastily yanking on his jeans, he rejoined the others just as Uncle Bert put the last of the sausages on to grill.

When they were cooked, and the inevitable billy of tea was stewing, Uncle Bert carefully cleared away the ashes and coals from part of the fire and uncovered a thick, disc-shaped object, black and charred all over.

'Here you are,' he said with a note of pride, 'genuine damper to go with the snags.' Holding it gingerly, because it was still hot even to his caloused hands, he carefully broke it open to reveal the white, scone-like interior, liberally studded with sultanas.

Jack and Sue grinned in anticipation. This was real bushman's tucker, something they had heard about all their lives, but never tasted. The smell of the newly-baked damper, the sausages, and the aromatic smoke from the burning gum leaves gave their appetites an edge they had not experienced before. They set to with a will. The sausages, seasoned with hearty dollops of tomato sauce, tasted even better than last night. The damper, although butterless, and (since Uncle Bert was no great shakes as a cook) slightly doughy in the middle, was eaten with gusto. Washed down with several mugs of tea it descended to lie, heavily but happily, on their unprotesting stomachs.

It didn't take long to tidy up the camp, pack their gear into the back of the ute, smother the fire, and be on their way again. Before they left, Jack rescued his underpants from the bonnet, and finished dressing.

They crossed the river, the bridge making a satisfying clattering as the car joggled the uneven planks. As they left it behind them, Uncle Bert remarked,

'That's the last permanent water I reckon we'll find until we get to the diggings. We should be all right there, though. It's a rocky outcrop, with two or three deep water-holes that are supposed never to dry up. Reckon they're twenty or thirty feet deep, and they say the Abos used to use the area as some sort of sacred tribal ground. So we should be right. The Abos knew what they were about.'

Jack nodded in agreement, but he and Sue were only half listening. Filled with good food, they were content to watch idly as the country sped past. Every few miles the scrub changed subtly and almost imperceptibly, but the earth itself varied more dramatically. The red soil would give way abruptly to a strip of black soil, and that, in turn to white. The change would be as sharp as if a giant had poured out streams of different coloured icings. Sometimes the humped saltbush would merge into a small gibber plain, where the stones were so thick it was difficult to see the soil between them, and where virtually nothing grew.

Yet even here there was life, and they often saw a stumpy-tail lizard waddling in slow progress across the road, or a goanna, flashy and defiant in his yellow and brown, would raise his head to stare at their oncoming car before scuttling off in a spurt of dust. Birds were scarce, but occasionally they would see emus in ones or twos, or even a small mob of half-grown young and one adult bird.

'They'd be males,' said Uncle Bert, pointing to the fully grown ones. 'The females only lay the eggs. Then they shoot through, leaving poor old dad to do the hatching and raise the chicks.'

Usually the emus would pound away as the car drew level, though sometimes one would pace alongside for a while before making a death-defying dash across their path for the apparently more attractive safety on the other side of the road, its plumage flopping up and down like a ridiculous feathered kilt above its absurdly naked thighs.

Once they came to a series of ridges crossing the road at right angles. By now the road had shrunk to a single lane, half-way between a track and a road, and it was a good thing that there were no other cars. The hillocks rose and fell abruptly, with no way of seeing over the crest of each ridge until you were actually there. It was rather like riding the Big Dipper switchback at a fun fair. At the foot and crest of each ridge the bulldust lay soft and unexpectedly thick, and several times Uncle Bert had to fight the wheel to prevent the ute going into a slide. If they came face to face with another car at a rest, there would be no way of avoiding an accident. Still, there wasn't much chance of that, for since leaving the river that morning they had passed only one other car in three hours, and that had been a Land-Rover with a couple of dogs aboard, obviously going out to muster a nearby paddock.

They left the hillocks behind them after about half an hour, and soon Uncle Bert slowed down.

'Turn-off's somewhere about here,' he said, 'but it's pretty hard to spot.'

For another half-hour or so they drove slowly, Uncle Bert peering from side to side, occasionally almost stopping, and now and again muttering directives to himself.

'Yeah, that big dead gum . . .'

'Don't remember that rock there.'

'Bit of pear building up around here. . .'

'Don't think I've passed it.'

'Shouldn't be far now, I reckon.'

'There she is!'

He turned triumphantly to Jack and Sue. 'You can't fool an old bushman, even after a dozen years,' he chuckled. Then, pointing to a few dark humps just visible on the

Anyway, I don't think he uses these back paddocks now unless he's pushed to in a real bad drought year. They're pretty good grazing.'

There was still another point worrying Jack.

'Shouldn't we have a miner's licence?'

'Yeah, well you should have one of those. But let's put it this way. Sometimes I go for months without doing any prospecting, other times, like now, I get on to something that may turn out to be pretty good. So I reckon it's better to go out and have a look-see. If she's useless, I haven't done me dough. If she's good, I'll head back into town, get a licence and a right to enter, and then put in a claim.'

'What if you get caught though?'

'Well, I never have, have I?' Uncle Bert chuckled. Then, seeing Jack's worried look, he added,

'It'll be okay. Mick Hanna's the bloke in charge, and he's an old mate of mine. And there's no point chucking good money down the drain if you don't know what you'll get back, is there?'

Sue joined in Uncle Bert's laughter, but Jack only gave a half-hearted smile. He might act up and play the fool, but that was only because it was better to be laughed at deliberately—that's if you were going to be laughed at anyway. But underneath the comic cut-ups lived a worrier, a stickler for doing-the-right-thing. It was, he supposed, some sort of reaction against his father's behaviour. Dad didn't seem to care what he did, or what people thought. But when Dad lay slobbering drunkenly in the gutter, Jack got a share of the blame. People didn't trust him. They told their kids, 'I wish you wouldn't mix with that Jack Clarke', just because he was Dan the Drunk's son. Old Drunken Dan, who lived a dirty disreputable life with all those women. A disgrace to the community!

Well, Jack had no intention of being a disgrace to the community. He had no illusions about being its shining light either. But at least, if he abided by the rules nobody could ever point at *him*. There were rules at school, and rules for crossing the road, and rules for delivering the papers, and Jack tried to follow them all. Within the rules lay safety and security, like that character in the comic strip with his blanket. If you knew what to do all the time, then there was no room for doubt or worry. If you obey the rules you can't go wrong, and if you don't go wrong, you can't be blamed or pointed out.

Jack was jolted out of his reverie by a violent explosion, a sudden cry from Sue, and a shouted 'What the hell!' from Uncle Bert. He had been vaguely aware for a while that they had been zigzagging along the edge of a deep cutaway as Uncle Bert searched for a reasonable slope where they could get across. The edge was smooth going, with very little timber or obstructions and they were making fair speed. Even as the sequence of noises sorted themselves out into an orderly array in Jack's mind which signalled 'tyre blow-out', the car slewed sickeningly around as Uncle Bert fought to bring it under control. A tree stump loomed up on their left as Uncle Bert spun the wheel frantically. Jack ducked as they headed straight for the stump. The near side mudguard struck a scrunching blow, and Jack was knocked forward. His head struck the side pillar of the windscreen and he half-crumpled to the floor. This probably saved his life, for otherwise he might have gone straight through the windscreen. The car bounced off the stump and smacked sharply to the right, its wheels almost on the edge of the cutaway. The bank collapsed and, like a clumsy swimmer, the ute dived forwards. Uncle Bert crashed on to the steering wheel, which snapped under the impact and threw him back against the seat. The ute dropped ten feet or so into the ravine, and landed on its front wheels. This second jolt threw Uncle Bert forwards once again on to the steering column. This time he didn't bounce back. He was conscious of a shearing, searing pain as he thought irrelevantly, 'What a way to start a holiday.' Then nothing more.

Sue, too terrified and shocked to scream, was hurled off the back seat and bruised and tumbled about on the floor. The car teetered for a moment on its nose, as if considering which way to fall, then flopped back on to its base. There were a few final tinkles of glass, and then a stunning silence.

Sue was the only one conscious, and she lay in the gloom on the floor for minutes, or maybe it was days. If she moved, perhaps it would all start up again. So she lay still, dazed and sore, and with a warm, salty taste in her mouth. Her nose was bleeding and she had bitten her tongue, but she was unaware of this. All she wanted was Uncle Bert to lean over and tell her everything was all right, and to hear his fat chuckle. Why didn't he say something? Why didn't Jack help her? Perhaps they'd both gone off to get help and forgotten all about her. No, they wouldn't be so mean and selfish. Perhaps they were both dead then. Oh, where were they, and what were they doing?

Fumbling, and scared of what she would find, Sue slowly raised herself off the floor and peered over into the front seat. There was Uncle Bert, his shoulders slumped forwards, his head hanging down towards his chest, the back of his neck looking strangely weak and helpless. Hesitantly Sue reached out a hand and touched his shoulder.

'Uncle Bert, Uncle Bert,' she said, and was surprised at the faint, husky sound of her voice. He didn't move, and she called again, louder this time. Only silence. Suddenly Sue wanted to pound at him with her fists, to hit the back of his hateful head until he was forced to answer, but she couldn't. She felt uncomfortable, rather like being in church. That feeling of being surrounded by some power that you didn't at all understand, so that even your thoughts went on tiptoe in case they disturbed things.

Sniffing miserably, Sue wiped her still bleeding nose and looked at Jack. He was crouched sideways on the floor as though trying to snatch a nap, one arm stretched along the seat towards Uncle Bert, and his right cheek resting on the edge of the seat, his head tilted slightly back. Sue stared at him in horror. His eyes were closed, his lips slightly parted, and there was a large grazed lump on his forehead where his head had connected with the windscreen pillar.

Still confused from the accident, Sue's thoughts took off along crazy tracks.

'He's asleep,' she thought dazedly. 'Trust Jack! Just when I need him, he decides to have a sleep. Fat lot of good he is . . . We must get help for Uncle Bert, and help for the car, and Jack should be doing it. He's a *boy* after all.' But even as she thought this, Sue was afraid that Jack awake might be little better than Jack asleep. He'd never take the . . . what was the word Mr Hawkins, the headmaster, was always talking about? The inin . . . invit . . . yes, that was it . . . the initiative. Mr Hawkins was a great one for initiative. Responsibility and leadership and initiative. He was always planning special class projects and outings to test the kids' initiative. People must be able to make decisions, solve problems, stand on their own two feet, use what was to hand. Like that puzzle about how to get on to an island without a bridge by using only three planks all of which were too short to reach it. To solve that sort of thing showed real initiative, Mr Hawkins said.

But Jack had no initiative, Sue had decided long ago, although then she was little, and hadn't known quite how to put it into words. Jack would run a mile from responsibility, and he never made decisions. Even on his paper run, if he was one paper short, he'd practically have a fit trying to decide what to do, and then he'd usually end up by going all the way back to the shop to see Mr Miles about it.

It was Sue who had thought up the places to hide their money. It was Sue who decided what to buy and when, and usually Jack just went along. Sue knew Jack had been upset by Uncle Bert's casual attitude to miner's licences. Jack was so stuffy, even though he could be the school comedian when he chose. The few times they went swimming in the town pool, Jack would get out right on six when the closing bell rang—not like the other kids who insisted on one last dive, and then another and another until Mr Backhouse practically had to chase them away. Yes, if there was a rule for any situation, then Jack would dig his heels in and insist on following it, no matter what. If there was a rule that said you had to test boiling water by putting your hand in it, I bet Jack would do it, Sue thought crossly.

And now, here they were, miles from anywhere, in a broken-down old car, and there were no rules to follow. So Jack went to sleep! Perhaps he thought that he'd wake up and find everything all right. He always went to bed whenever things went wrong. Just lay there, curled up, sometimes asleep, but more often just staring bleakly across their dusty yards.

Sue felt angrier and angrier, for she was terribly afraid.

'I'll make him wake up and help me,' she thought.

Leaning over the back of the seat, she gave him a hard slap on the shoulder.

'Jack!' she yelled. 'Jack! Jack, wake up!'

All that happened was that his head slumped forwards, his hair falling over his face. Sue's anger drained away as though someone had suddenly pulled a plug out of the soles of her feet. Fear leaped in her brain like an electric spark, and she hit at Jack wildly. Jack's head bobbed and lurched aimlessly as she thumped and shook him, and through her terror she could hear someone screaming 'Jack! Jack! Jack!' Then the sound of the screams changed to sobs, great gulping choking paroxysms that shook her whole body, and she knew that the screams and the sobs were her own.

Frantically she began to struggle with the door handle. They were both dead, Jack and Uncle Bert, and she wanted to get out of the car and run and run and run, wildly, until she was miles away and safe. She didn't want to stay here and die, all alone, in the bush. If only she could get out and run, there would be someone. She would run all the way home, wherever it was. Or someone would save her. Or if she called loudly enough, someone would hear.

But the door wouldn't budge. Sue kicked and beat at it

until her fists were bruised, sobbing and gasping and calling out to Jack and Uncle Bert, and only dimly aware of what she was doing. The heat inside the car, and her own shock and exhaustion gradually lessened her frenzy. Finally she collapsed limply, her hands still grasping the door handle, and sobbed soundlessly. Worn out and numb, she decided that if she was going to die, she might as well die now and be done with it. Dull with fatigue and despair, she sat back, then crawled full length on to the seat, pillowed her head in the crook of one arm, and lay there, whimpering quietly from time to time.

It couldn't take long to die, surely, once you'd made your mind up.

She was still waiting when Jack recovered consciousness, stuck his head over the seat back, and said, 'It's all right, Sue.' For a moment she was even a bit disappointed. Lying there waiting for death had been so simple once she'd accepted it, but now everything was going to start all over again. And she, Sue, would have to cope, because Jack couldn't.

As quickly, she felt ashamed of herself. She was twelve years old, and girls of her age didn't die. Oh, sometimes little babies did, and old people did, and occasionally people who were very sick in hospital did (like Mum), and now and again children got drowned, or run over, or killed in accidents. But she was Sue Clarke, who *wasn't* killed in an accident, and neither was her brother. And if Jack was fine, then Uncle Bert would be too; he'd just been knocked out like Jack had.

Between them, it would all come right!

CHAPTER FOUR

The past merged into the present, and Sue was kneeling beside Jack. On each side, and only about thirty feet apart, rose the crumbling red walls of the cutting. They were gnarled and studded with pebbles, straggly tufts of grass clung tenaciously to their soil giving an untidy moth-eaten effect, and clumps of saltbush and wild hops were scattered about the ground. Beside them stood the ute, battered, scratched and useless, and canted slightly to one side. Within the ute sat . . . but that didn't yet bear thinking about.

The heat was an immense oppressive stillness, a furnace, a solid way that you could slice through. Every movement was a physical effort, and the very air resisted you. Already Jack's sweat-soaked clothes were dry, and his throat was dry, dry and rasping as the desiccated clay of the gully. He still lay on the ground, and he and Sue looked at one another, hazel eyes and blue, seeing and not seeing, their minds and bodies exhausted.

'I've got to get a drink of water,' Jack croaked, and half sat up.

'No, I'll go.'

Sue went round to the back of the ute, keeping as far away from the car and its ghastly passenger as possible, and returned shortly with a mug full of water. Jack took a mouthful, rinsed it around his mouth and spat it out, then drained the rest in great gulps.

'That's better. Thanks, Sue.'

Sue squatted down beside him, and again they were silent. She pulled at the leaves of a small bush.

'Jack . . . what are we going to do?'

'I dunno.'

Jack picked up a stick and drew a square in the dust,

pressing with such force that the stick bent and then snapped. A small brown ant, scurrying along a zigzag route with purposeless busy-ness fell into the deep groove made by the stick, and scrabbled frantically to get out, but the soft dust continually collapsed under its weight and sent it tumbling back. Undeterred, it tried again and again. Jack watched the ant's movements. Stupid thing, doesn't it know it'll keep on falling! His gaze shifted slightly, and he became aware of the broken piece of stick still stuck in the soil, its jagged splintered end like . . . like . . . in the car. His hand swept out and knocked the stick flying. Then he savagely scrubbed the sand smooth, obliterating square and ant.

'We'll stay here till we're rescued.'

'Here?' Sue's eyes widened. 'But nobody knows where we are and—and we'll be gone for weeks before they even know we're missing.'

'Rats!' replied Jack roughly. 'The Greek at the café knows where we were heading for a start. We've got plenty of water and some food—'

Sue interrupted.

'But what about . . . ?' She found she couldn't say 'Uncle Bert'. Her mouth was dry and her throat tightened up. 'What about . . . him?' she whispered, jerking her head towards the car.

'Well, what else *can* we do?' exploded Jack.

'Couldn't we get back to the road, or the hills?'

'That's the dopiest thing you've said yet. The road's miles and miles away. Anyway, I don't even know what direction it's in.'

'We could follow the car tracks.'

'Yeah? Well you'd need to be a blacktracker to follow them. And even if you could, it must be nearly forty miles, the way we twisted about coming in from the gate.'

'Okay, but why can't we go on to the mountains then? There's waterholes there. *He* said so,' Sue continued desperately.

'I told you!' Jack yelled. 'We've got plenty of water.

We're staying here. You've *got* to camp by your car if anything happens.'

'I don't see why.' Sue was stubborn and sullen.

'Because you die if you don't. Look at that family up the Birdsville Track. They only went a couple of miles away and they all died. The whole family *and* their dog.'

Jack's face was white beneath the grime, and his eyes were hating Sue as he glared at her.

Behind the hatred lay fear. Fear of not knowing what to do. Hatred, suddenly, of the vast, bleached bush around them. It lay silent in the noonday heat, yet seemed to hum and pulsate as though a hidden dynamo were vibrating just out of earshot. Dirty, stinking, hot, horrid *bloody* country. Fear of what was in the front seat. Fear and a choking nausea when he thought of what the days could bring . . . and the summer heat. There was only one thing Jack was sure of about their present situation, and that was that you stayed with the car until you were rescued. No matter what. There was fear, too, because a tiny part of himself kept insisting that perhaps that wasn't the perfect answer. Perhaps this time they should break the rules. Perhaps in two or three weeks when they were found—if they were found—it would be too late.

Jack wondered if the ute could be seen from the air. He thought not. There were a few scrubby trees overhanging the gully, and the car would be partly concealed. Had Uncle Bert followed a regular route in from the gate or were there other ways? Did he just drive in the general direction, skirting trees and obstacles as best he could. How many other people knew this track? If it took Uncle Bert so much trouble to find the gate in the first place, would anyone else be able to find it? What did they do when people were lost? Jack tried to think, but his mind was all mixed up. He vaguely seemed to remember that Air Force planes were used. Bits of old news items dimly recalled. Or was that only over the sea? Well, Air Force planes would never spot them. A helicopter might. We must make a plan. He tried to remember what he had read in books and magazines, and seen at the pictures about castaways.

As though reading his thoughts, Sue broke in,

'Jack! We've got to do *something*. We can't just sit here. Look, shouldn't we . . . shouldn't we . . . I mean . . . about *him*? We can't just leave him there . . . in the car.'

Jack stared at Sue. Why was she always putting it all on him? Why couldn't she just shut up and leave him alone?

'Jack?'

'Sue, we can't!' His face twisted with agony and grief. 'We ought to, but we can't. We couldn't get him off the . . . out. *We can't*! WE CAN'T!'

'Oh!' Sue's lips shaped the word, but no sound came. Her eyes filled with tears.

'Oh, for heaven's sake!' yelled Jack. 'Are you going to sit around all day long crying? A fat lot've good that'll do.'

Then, as Sue looked at him, stricken, he said more quietly, 'Look, I'm trying to think things out. It's awful, *I* know, Sue. But we're stuck here, and we've got to try and find a way to work it out.'

'We could move away . . .' began Sue.

'Oh, don't start that again . . .'

'No,' interruted Sue as she saw Jack's temper beginning to rise. 'I didn't mean right away. Just a little bit away, you know, down the gully. Find a spot where it's flat and sheltered, and take what we need from the car, but just be a little bit away from . . . *it*.'

Jack gazed at Sue with dawning admiration. It would solve most of their problems. They'd still be near enough to be rescued, but far enough away not to have to suffer from . . . well, from whatever happened.

'Right,' he said, standing up slowly and dusting his palms down his jeans. 'I'll go and find a spot this way, and you can go the other way.'

Sue stood up too.

'No,' she said, her face set, 'I'm coming with you.'

Heck, thought Jack disgustedly. Just when you thought a

girl was coming good, she had to go and ruin it by being silly.

'But it'll be quicker if we go separately,' he countered.

'I don't care. Anyway, it might be weeks before we're found, so we've plenty of time. And I don't want to be alone.'

Jack remembered Sue's face as he had seen it when he first recovered consciousness after the accident. He didn't know how long he'd been out—perhaps for an hour or more—and all that time Sue had been afraid they'd both been dead. That was an awful time to have gone through.

'Okay,' he said contritely, 'let's go this way first.'

They headed back up the gully the way they had originally come before the crash. After about fifty yards the gully curved left, and as Jack and Sue rounded the curve they were halted by a huge tangle of debris. A small tree had collapsed across the gully and every couple of years, when there was sufficient rain, further flotsam was carried down to pile up in a matted barricade.

Sue poked around at the side, and began to scramble her way over, half on the bank and half on the tangle of old bushes, scraps of timber, fencing wire and bits of paper.

'I think there's a way over here,' she called.

'Don't be silly, Sue. We can't lug all the stuff we need past all this rubbish.'

'But it looks much clearer over the other side.'

'No, it's no use. We'll have to go back.'

Reluctantly Sue turned and jumped down, landing awkwardly and stumbling on to her knees.

'You all right?'

'Yes,' she stood up, 'just a bit shaky.' She brushed her knees clean, wincing slightly. Then she balanced one foot against the side of the gully, and inspected her left knee more closely, stretching the skin carefully.

'It's bleeding,' she said, and watched with satisfaction as a tiny drop of blood oozed to the surface. Jack stood by impatiently.

'You'll live,' he said scornfully. 'Oh, come *on*, Sue. It

must be getting late, and we've got to find a possie and get settled before dark.'

Jack turned and strode back the way they had come. Sue hurried after him, limping slightly for the first few steps until the stinging stopped. They slowed down as they neared the car again, and its silent driver, then hurried past and explored the forward part of the gully. At this end the gully wound and twisted almost continuously, and after the third bend they found what they were looking for. A gum tree on the bank gave partial shade, and they could always climb out once they were settled if it got too hot. More importantly, for some reason the weeds and shrubs which choked much of the rest of the bed had decided not to grow here. There was a bare patch of sand and pebbles almost the whole width of the washaway, and about twenty feet long.

'This'll do,' Jack decided after inspecting it briefly. 'Now we want to bring back everything we need—food—water—and whatever else we find that might come in handy.'

Feeling slightly more cheerful at having a definite plan and a definite activity, they turned back to the car. The bonnet of the utility was facing them as they rounded the final bend, and, as they appeared, a pair of crows perched on it flapped slowly off, cawing sardonically.

'Oh God, no,' groaned Jack.

'What?'

'Those crows. We'll have to wind the windows up.'

Sue's face whitened as she understood what Jack was saying. She knew the stories the kids told, tales that were common knowledge: of crows attacking weakened lambs, pecking their eyes out, killing them, feeding on rotting corpses. Jack picked up a handful of stones and hurled them at the crows, which had taken refuge in a nearby tree. The stones fell short of their target, and the crows merely raised their wings slightly and watched with malevolent interest. In a fury of despair and rage Jack ran at the bank. Somehow he managed to claw his way to the top, where he hurled himself at the tree, beating at its trunk with his clenched fists.

'Get to hell!' he screamed, beating and pounding and screaming until the crows, tired of all the fuss, took off and circled slowly overhead. Jack collapsed at the foot of the tree, tears streaming down his face. He couldn't do it; it wasn't fair. This was their first holiday ever, and it was horrible, *horrible*, HORRIBLE. Sue was right. They'd never be found if they stayed, but he didn't know where to go. They'd die if they stayed, and they'd die if they went, and the crows would get them. In a wave of self-pity and weakness, Jack saw their bones bleaching, half-covered by drifting sand and tussock grass. It happened all the time, not only to new chums, but to experienced bushmen. He and Sue were only kids; there was nothing they could do. As if in agreement, the crows settled back in the tree, and sat there, prepared to wait forever.

Jack didn't know how much later it was that Sue's head appeared as she clambered slowly over the edge of the gully, pulling herself carefully up by clumps of grass. She went over and touched Jack hesitantly on the shoulder. Without being able to put it into words, she was aware of most of Jack's present emotions. She felt his fear, for she was just as afraid, but she knew too that Jack had all the responsibility. She could turn to him, lean on him, and ask him for comfort; but he was all alone. He'd always been alone, even in a crowd. She and Jack had never been very close, had never confided in one another. He couldn't turn to her and ask for help. He had to be the leader now, when he had always been a follower.

'Come on, Jack. Let's start right away and do it all together.'

Slowly Jack rose to his feet and followed Sue to the edge of the gully.

'Along here,' she indicated, 'it's an easier way down.'

She led him to the spot where she had clambered up. It was here that the utility had plunged over the edge, and in doing so had broken loose some of the earth in a miniature avalanche that sloped slightly instead of being as steep as the rest of the walls. Slipping and skidding on palms, heels and bottoms, they followed one another down, arriving in a cloud of dust and a scattering of small stones.

'Let's . . . let's do the windows first,' Sue offered.

'I'll do them,' Jack muttered, turning abruptly. 'You stay here.'

He walked around to the near side door, pulled it open, and wound the window up. Then he closed the two back seat windows, though to do the near side one he had to stretch across the back seat. Finally, clenching his teeth, and compressing his lips until they formed a white slit across his face, he opened the driver's door.

It might have been the joggling and slamming of doors, or it might have been a matter of pressures and balances, but as Jack opened the door his uncle's right hand slipped and fell down beside the seat, the arm fully extended. Jack stared at it in horror. He couldn't close the door while that arm was still there. His eyes were fixed rigidly on the hand, refusing to look at anything else. His heart was pounding and he swallowed spasmodically, trying not to be sick. As if in a trance, he put his own hand out, slowly, slowly, and touched that of his uncle. Carefully, even gently, his fingers closed around the rough palm, he picked it up, and placed it tenderly across the dead man's knees. It felt strangely warm, not cold and clammy as he had expected; his mind registered the fact automatically. His eyes flickered over the dashboard and glove box. There was a box of matches there, which he reached out and pocketed. Nothing else. He wound the window up, shut the quarter vent which had been open, and almost reverently closed the car door.

Somehow, by touching and rearranging the body, he felt that a ritual had been accomplished. He hadn't just left him there, but had made a gesture of respect and farewell. Even his fear had left him now, and he felt that nothing more could ever quite touch him again. Uncle Bert was dead, but he was peaceful and happy in death. He'd harmed no one while he was alive, and could hurt no one now he was dead. They could leave him here, in the coffin of his car, and he wouldn't mind. Jack let out his breath in an unconscious sigh of relief. Whatever the future would bring, the worst was over.

Jack turned towards Sue and smiled—a smile quite unlike his usual cocky grin.

'Come on,' he said, 'let's start unloading.'

Jack undid the chain and bolt holding the tailgate up. At first it stuck, but after a few hard thumps that made his fist tingle it dropped down, forming a small horizontal ledge supported by its corner chains. Everything inside was tumbled about higgledy-piggledy. One water drum was still upright—the one Sue had used—but the other had fallen on its side and rolled forwards, tearing open the neck of the flourbag, and bursting the remaining packets of dried fruits. The axe, Uncle Bert's prized rifle, cartridges which had scattered out of their box, the blackened billy, plates, a squashed orange, spare groundsheets and blankets, sprawled in total confusion, all covered with a dusting of white which had puffed out of the flourbag at the moment of impact. Over everything buzzed the ever-present flies, sucking up the juice from the oozing sultanas, and tramping stickily from one patch of food to the next.

'We'll just have to get everything out as best we can,' sighed Jack, 'and then see what's usable.'

He 'walked' the partly empty water drum to the edge of the tailboard and tried to ease it to the ground, but it was too heavy, and fell with a thunk. Sue hauled at the bag of flour, and dumped it beside the drum.

'What'll we do? Pull everything out first, and then move it?'

'I dunno.' Jack thought for a minute, his face already flushed and beaded with sweat from his exertions in the burning heat. 'Perhaps we'd better cart each bit off as we get it out, otherwise we won't be able to move if we end up with all this stuff under our feet.'

Sue went to lift the flour, but its weight made her stagger.

'Here,' said Jack, 'I'll take that. You roll the water

drum.' So with Jack shouldering the flourbag and Sue, bent double, rolling and steering the drum as it jolted its contrary way along, they made the first of many trips. Each time they returned, unloaded, sorted, and loaded up for the next. Already the sun was low, a sign that soon the short, semi-tropical twilight would be upon them, and then the night. Sometimes they found they could only carry one or two things at a time, as many of the articles were awkwardly shaped, or half broken open. After a couple of trips, Jack leaned against the tailgate briefly to catch his breath.

'This is too slow,' he said worriedly, 'we'll never be through by dark.' He stared thoughtfully at the pile of stuff that still remained.

'I'll tell you what, Sue! Where are the blankets? Have you taken them along yet?'

'No, they're here.' Sue dragged them out and shook a cloud of flour and dust off them.

'Well,' continued Jack, 'suppose you do the unloading and sorting, and put all the stuff that's okay on to one of the blankets. Then I'll shift it down to the camp while you load up the other one. That should speed things up a bit.'

'That's a beaut idea.' Sue was surprised by Jack's quick thinking. Perhaps he was going to come good after all.

With renewed energy they set to, piling all the equipment they could into the centre of the first blanket, which Jack had spread out on the ground.

'Hey, hold on,' cried Jack, as the pile mounted. 'I've got to be able to carry it. Save the rest up for the next load.'

Sue retrieved the packets of sugar which she had just dropped on the blanket, and stood back. Jack gathered up the four corners and twisted them roughly in the middle to make a crude sack. Grunting, he heaved it up and swung it over his back.

'Can you manage?'

'Yeah, it's not too bad,' Jack replied. 'At least it'll be quicker this way.' It was, in fact, a fairly light load, but its bumpy shape made it awkward to balance. In addition, Jack found that unsuspected corners and knobs jabbed into his back as the makeshift sack swung and bounced. Once the blanket caught on a bit of bush as he walked past and something, it may have been the prongs of a fork, gave him a mighty jab. Still, by the time he had dumped his load along the gully and returned, Sue had the second blanket almost ready, and Jack reckoned they had probably cut the time for each trip by more than half.

After several more trips very little remained except for the untouched drum of water, and the loose cartridges which Sue was busily collecting and dropping back into their box. With relief, Jack shouldered his final bundle and turned away. Sue collected the last of the cartridges, then ran her hand carefully over the floor of the ute to make sure none had rolled, unseen, into the corners. No, they were all found.

She watched Jack disappear around the first bend, looking, she thought, like some particularly down-at-heel swaggie. With a sigh she wiped her hair back from her face, where it was stuck and matted with sweat. Sue didn't believe she had ever felt so hot before in all her life. She would *die* if she didn't have a drink of water. It was a pity Jack had taken the mugs—or had he? Suddenly Sue was sure the second mug, the one she had used to take Jack a drink earlier, was still where they had left it beside the car. She trotted over to investigate. Yes, there it was, lying on its side in the dust. Sue picked it up, and as she turned to come back, she spotted the canvas waterbag strapped to the front of the car. It was bone dry and empty, but she knew Jack would want to have it; at least it would give them cool water during the worst of the day. She unstrapped it and carried it around to the back of the car. Then she reached in to roll the water drum forward, but she could only just reach it. Sue looked back to see if Jack was coming, but he was nowhere in sight.

She scrambled carefully on to the tailgate, which creaked protestingly under her, and for a moment she wondered anxiously if the chains would hold. But they were strong enough to take more than her slight weight. Crouching down she inched forward to the drum. Struggling and straining, she finally managed to roll it towards her. Once she got it started it came easily, for the car was tilted at a slight angle. Fortunately, the drum caught in the wide crack between the rear of the car and the tailgate, or else it might have rolled right off. Sue was able to leave it balanced there while she jumped back on to the ground. There was still no sign of Jack, so Sue heaved and pulled until, with a final jerk, she managed to lurch the drum up on to its end. She unscrewed the cap, put it carefully beside the drum, and picked up the mug. Using her body as a brace to prevent the drum tipping right over and spilling, Sue carefully tilted it inch by inch, until a trickle of water began to run out of the opening and around the rim. With relief she held her mug in position and steered the trickle into it.

It was at that moment that the bull ant bit her. Bull ants, a primitive species, live in a state of almost perpetual frenzied hatred. Their first reaction to every situation is 'Bite it and see'. In fact, a favourite pastime with country children is to stir up a bull ants' nest with a stick, then leap back and watch the ants come boiling out. This particular ant, scrambling home late after an afternoon of frantic reconnaissance, found its usual path blocked by a large lump of rubber thong, surmounted by a chunk of tasty-looking foot. Ever on the alert, and even more short-tempered than usual, the ant sank its pincers deep into Sue's instep.

Sue screamed and jumped back. The drum, its support gone, teetered precariously for a moment and fell with a thud, turning over so that its opening landed on the ground. The rim of the drum landed squarely on Sue's foot.

'Jack! Jack!' she screamed, just as Jack came into sight.

Jack broke into a run and reached her side in seconds. His first thought was the water, and he quickly up-ended the drum, but he could tell from its weight and the ease with which he shifted it, that it was too late. Sue was writhing about on the ground, her legs clenched between her arms, and moaning with pain. The first shock of the accident had passed, and the bruised and crushed nerves were sending searing flashes of agony that made Sue rock from side to side in an attempt to escape from them. Jack hunkered down beside her and tried to hold her still, so that he could examine her foot.

Only the surface of the skin was slightly grazed, but already an ugly, crescent-shaped lump was rising. It curved in an arc from her big toe to her little toe, and it was stained with rust from the rim of the drum. Jack put his arm around Sue and held her tight, hoping to squeeze some of the pain out. He remembered the time he had jammed his fingers in the door. Being held tight and tense within himself had seemed to help. Later, they'd discovered that his little finger was broken, and he'd had to wear it splinted up for weeks.

'Oh, God! he thought, don't let Sue's foot be broken. One part of his mind wondered idly how easily could bones break? And how much would a 44-gallon drum weigh?

'Sue, Sue,' he said urgently, 'can you walk on it?'

'I . . . don't . . . know.' Sue's words came stiffly, holding herself taut against the pain.

'Well, wiggle your toes.'

'I . . . can't. It hurts too much.'

'Let me try, then.' Gently he reached down, and slipped Sue's thong off. Sue clutched her foot tightly around the instep and winced away from Jack's hand. Jack touched her toes.

'Don't . . . don't! It'll hurt!' she cried.

Carefully Jack tried to move her toes up and down, but Sue cried out with pain, and grabbed her foot away.

'Did that hurt?'

'Yes.'

'A lot?'

'Yes.'

Jack sat back, and put his arm around Sue's thin shoulders again. He couldn't really tell, he thought. If Sue's foot is broken, we're done for. Even the loss of the water was forgotten in this new worry. His eyes focused on the rim of the gully, and he realized with a start that the sun had gone down.

'Sue,' he said, 'we've got to get back to the camp. Come on, I'll help you.'

He jumped to his feet, and put his hands out for Sue's. Her eyes looked at him dully, clouded with pain and despair. He bent down and loosened Sue's hands, which still grasped her foot, then he leaned back to draw her to her feet. Unsteadily and awkwardly Sue strained to stand up, then stood swaying, her left leg well bent to keep her injured foot off the ground. Steadying her with one hand, Jack retrieved her thong.

'I'll come back for the other stuff after. Here, put your arm around my neck and hop.' Jack slid his right arm around Sue's waist. 'Come on, it's not far.'

Sue gave a tentative hop, and then another. Jack found it almost impossible to support her properly, or to match his steps with Sue's hops, but slowly and lurchingly they moved forwards. Sue gave a stifled cry as each hop sent a new thrill of agony jarring up her foot.

They had to rest several times on the way, but finally they came to the camp site, where the salvage from the car lay, still in disorder. Propping Sue against the side of the bank for a moment, Jack quickly smoothed out one of the blankets, and helped Sue over to it. With a moan of relief she sank down, then gingerly lowered her foot till the heel was resting on the ground. Her body was trembling with strain and shock; she felt sick and completely spent.

Jack used the rest of the daylight in an attempt to sort out the stores and put them to one side, and in gathering some wood for a fire. He used several matches before he could get the clump of dry grass and twigs burning sufficiently to catch the larger sticks. The billy seemed to take forever to boil, and once he had to go off into the gloom for more wood. He opened a tin of camp pie, poured a mug of tea, milked and sugared it well, and handed it to Sue. She shook her head numbly.

'You must eat something,' he insisted.

Sue took a sip of tea, and suddenly was ravenously hungry. She dug out a spoonful of the tinned meat and put it in her mouth. Immediately she felt nauseated. Her mouth was dry as chaff, and she rolled the meat round and round before she was able to force it down. Then she shook her head and handed the tin back to Jack.

'Come on, Sue, try a bit more.' He spooned out a tiny lump and passed it over to her. Sue took it, but found she couldn't force it down.

'I'll be sick if I eat anything more.'

'Well, drink your tea, then.'

Sue took another sip, and found that it was just what she needed. It had a smooth hot richness from the condensed milk, and seemed to fill every corner of her aching body with a beautiful relaxing warmth. The mug empty, she lay back on the blanket. Jack watched her with concern.

'Try to go to sleep, Sue. I'll fix up everything here.' He folded the side of the blanket over her, and rolled a second blanket up and put it under her head.

For a few minutes Sue watched him by the light of the fire. He finished off the tin of meat, drank his tea, and cleaned up half-heartedly. The throbbing in Sue's foot had changed to a dull ache, and she tossed over on to her back, trying to get comfortable. The sky was clear and cloudless, but the stars, so warm and welcoming only last night, seemed to prickle coldly and hatefully, as though snickering at her plight.

'They're glad,' thought Sue, and fell asleep, exhausted.

When he saw that Sue's eyes had closed, Jack went over to the remaining water drum. Cautiously he tapped its sides, trying to tell from the sound how much was left. But wherever he tapped it, it sounded the same, and he was afraid to tap louder for fear of waking Sue. Quietly he moved away and, after a bit of searching, found a length of stick. He unscrewed the cap and pushed the stick in until he felt it touch the bottom. Pulling it out again, he took it nearer the fire. The bottom ten inches were dark and wet. Only enough water for a couple of days, he guessed.

He dropped down near Sue, and brooded into the fire.

They must get water. But where? Where? Where? The car radiator? Perhaps. But hadn't some fellow died once from the anti-rust compound in his radiator? Did Uncle Bert use anti-rust? he wondered. No, it was too risky to try it.

Perhaps Sue was right. They'd have to move. But where? The hills they had been heading for couldn't be more than a dozen miles away, perhaps even less, but how could they get there if Sue couldn't walk? And which direction were they in? Somewhere over to the left, he thought. He tried to recall the bits and pieces of bush lore and legend that he had been hearing all his life. You could tell from birds. They flew towards water at night and away from it in the morning. Or was it the other way round? Jack wasn't sure. He could shin up a tree in the morning. He should be able to see the hills from up high. He'd have to go through their provisions and see what they could take with them. If Sue was all right in the morning, it mightn't be impossible. Of course, they might become hopelessly lost and die anyway. But they couldn't stay where they were. Not now. Not without water. There was no choice, really.

Once the decision was reached, Jack felt relieved. It wasn't his decision, it had been forced on him. But a definite course of action was better than not knowing. In the morning, he'd make plans . . . tea . . . matches . . . Uncle Bert's gun? . . . His eyelids drooped, and Jack drifted off to sleep in the middle of his inventory.

CHAPTER FIVE

Jack slept heavily, his mind and body bruised by the shattering assaults of the terrible day, but his sleep was disturbed by confused and menacing dreams, so that he woke early and lay there, aware of an oppressive sense of foreboding. Sue, too, had spent a restless night, half-way between deep slumber and dozing, as the pain of her foot continually jolted her awake.

They both stirred shortly after piccaninny dawn and lay there absorbed in their own thoughts as the events of yesterday seeped slowly back into their minds. Already the sharp edge of horror had been slightly dulled, and there was even a certain exhilaration in the Robinson Crusoe-like adventure of the situation.

To be responsible for their own survival, without adults, and without help, was part of the universal dream of childhood. Despite the life-and-death stakes, it had the quality of a game, for it was impossible to imagine their own deaths. They saw death as a word, not even, with the ghastly, spitted memory of Uncle Bert before them, as a likely reality. Their minds, perhaps, saw themselves lying, still and shrivelled under the sun, but it was a Babes-in-the-Wood vision. When found, they would be able, as observers, to slip back into their bodies and return to life. Like most people, Jack and Sue existed on two levels. The important one, which influenced everything they did, was the real world of what was happening here and now. The equally real world of what was *likely* to happen was only a story book place, and could be altered if they thought about it hard enough. They could not truly believe in personal death and disaster, because they could not experience it before it happened. Their minds refused to listen when a faint voice whispered, 'It could be true.' No, only this gully was true.

It was only an adventure, and as exciting as that of any shipwrecked Swiss Family Robinson.

Eager to be on the move, Jack and Sue sat up almost simultaneously.

Chaos met their eyes.

The jumbled piles of salvage, which Jack thought he had stacked fairly neatly last night, seemed to have shifted during the dark into one messy hotchpotch. Small night animals had made quick nervous forays amongst the heaps, pushing and scraping with busy inquisitive snouts and paws. Whole armies of ants and squadrons of flies had spread the good news at the crack of dawn, and were now frantically raiding all the available food.

Jack leaped to his feet and raced to the rescue. Sue tried to follow him, but found she still couldn't put any weight on her foot, and sat down again on the blanket. Jack scurried about, brushing marauding ants off the sugar bag and hanging it from a tree, and gathering the rest of the food into a central pile which he dumped on to his blanket.

It was only then he realized that Sue was still sitting down.

'Come on, give us a hand.'

'I can't, my foot's too sore.'

'Oh no! Are you sure?'

Sue nodded.

Jack squatted down beside her, his eyes dark with concern. Here was a problem to be faced which he had hoped would disappear if he didn't think about it.

'Look,' he said, 'I'll get us something to eat, and perhaps you'll feel better then.'

Sue nodded again, but without much conviction.

Jack turned away and squirrelled through the pile of food. He found the remains of a loaf of bread, now almost as dry and hard as toast, and hacked it into rough slices. A few determined ants and flies were still mining in the jam tin. Jack shooed the flies away, and gave the tin a couple of thumps, which dislodged most of the ants, and a large portion of jam as well. He scraped out the last few ants with his finger, licked his finger and wiped it on the blanket, and then spread the last of the jam thickly on the bread. There was one large bottle of lemonade and three cans of beer, and Jack deftly flipped the top off the lemonade.

'Here,' he offered it to Sue, 'we'd better have this now. It'll save water and be less to carry. Anyway, we'll have to get cracking as soon as possible, before it's too hot, so I don't want to waste time making a fire for tea.'

Sue accepted the bottle gratefully. The lemonade was warm and sickly sweet, but it helped to wash down the dry bread and jam. When she had finished, it was true, she did feel better, for it was the first food she'd had for twenty-four hours. But an attempt to walk brought a sharp stab of pain. Sue tried desperately, but even hobbling along on her heel, with the rest of her foot off the ground, proved too painful. Trust Jack to decide to move just when she couldn't walk, Sue thought crossly. Then, immediately, she felt ashamed for failing him when he needed her most.

Sue lowered herself dejectedly to the ground again, and Jack joined her. She was afraid to look at him, though, because of the defeat she might see in his eyes. But Jack was not defeated. He took Sue's hand to give her what comfort he could. He had never before been so aware of her, as a person, as a part of him. He sensed, gratefully, how hard she was trying to please him and felt, for the first time in his life, the strength of being needed. It was frightening—the awful responsibility, the risk of making the wrong decisions. But it was a calm kind of fear, he decided, not the sort that makes you all churned up inside. This skinny, worried-looking kid sister was *his* sister. They were alone together, yet not completely alone. Somehow they would succeed.

Jack squeezed Sue's hand, willing her to look at him.

'We *have* to go, you know that, Sue. We haven't enough water for more than a couple of days. I checked last night after you were asleep. Besides, no one will even think of looking for us in under a week at the least. Uncle Bert said there was permanent water in the rock holes in the hills, so we've got to find them. *Somehow* we've got to get there.'

Sue nodded. He hadn't roused on her, hadn't said a word about her spilling the water, or that it had been all her fault just because she couldn't wait a little bit longer for a drink.

'I could hop if you helped me.'

Jack thought of their blundering progress to the camp site and shook his head.

'No, it'd be too hard. Besides, I'll have to carry some food and all the water I can.'

'How about crutches?'

'Gee, that might work! I could find a couple of branches and make some.'

'How far is it?'

'I'm not sure. Look, you stay here and I'll climb up a tree and see if I can spot the hills. And while I'm doing that, could you go through the food and sort out what you reckon we ought to take and put it in a separate bundle?'

'Okay.' Sue was glad to have something useful to do.

Jack sped off, and Sue crawled her way over to the food blanket on her hands and knees, keeping her injured foot carefully off the ground. Pebbles and twigs cut into her knees, but she was determined not to give in. Really, apart from a continual nagging ache, her foot wasn't too bad, so long as she didn't stand on it or bump it, and Sue was sure she could make the trip to the hills. She had to.

Jack, meanwhile, had climbed out of the gully, and was scrambling up the only reasonably tall tree amongst the stunted shrubs. It was hard going, for the trunk was smooth and unbroken for nearly twelve feet. But Jack was a pretty good climber and, by gripping hard with knees, soles and arms, he managed to drag himself up to the first fork. Even at this low height he had an almost uninterrupted view of the whole plain. He turned his head slowly, following the horizon and there, in the distance, were a series of small humps which could only be the hills. Just about due west he reckoned, for the early morning sun was now right behind him. That was a stroke of luck, because now they'd only have to keep the sun on their backs in the morning, and on their faces in the afternoon. If it'd been something tricky like north-west, they could've really been in strife trying to keep in the right direction.

Jack felt more cheerful as he scraped his way down the trunk. Head west, and only about five miles, he hoped. He wasn't too sure of the exact distance, but he seemed to remember that it was supposed to be five miles to the horizon from eye level. Of course, he was up the tree when he saw them, and he didn't know how much farther that would make it. On the other hand, they'd been able to see the hills when they turned off the road yesterday. There was no guarantee, he thought, that they'd been driving straight at them; in fact the track was as crooked as a snake, but they'd hardly be *farther* away. Yes, Jack decided, five miles would be about right.

He slid down into the gully in the usual shower of loose earth and stones. Sue had been working well while he was gone. Although some of the heavier stores had defeated her, she had divided the rest into two fair-sized heaps.

'This is the one to take, and this is the stuff we don't want,' she pointed. 'Did you find the way?'

'Uh-uh! It's only about five miles, and straight to the west.'

Jack dropped down beside Sue and examined the two heaps of food. The one they were leaving was fine, but there seemed an awful lot in the other one. He sorted through the items carefully. There was sugar, at least half-a-dozen large tins of stew or baked beans, sultanas, tea, raisins, powdered and condensed milk, flour, a battered-looking unopened sliced loaf, an old golden syrup tin full of dripping, and three withered oranges. As well, there was the billy, frying pan, plates and mugs, and knives and forks. There would also be water to carry, and anything else they might discover, such as Uncle Bert's gun, which Jack had already decided to take. After all, they could be stuck in the hills for weeks, and they'd need food. The thought of shooting and skinning a roo didn't particularly appeal to Jack: he wasn't even sure how to go about it, so he pushed those details to the back of his mind. He'd face them when he came to them.

'We can't possibly carry all this stuff, Sue. We'll have to halve it at least.'

'Yes, well, I thought it'd be too much. But I just put in all the possibles so that we could decide when we saw them.'

'That was the right idea,' agreed Jack. 'Now, what can we chuck? Do you want the tea?'

'Not specially. Anyway, then you've got to take sugar and milk, too.'

'Okay. Tea's out. Now, what about all these tins? They weigh a ton.'

'But we've got to eat something.'

'I know. But whatever we take won't be enough for the time we might be there. I think we should just take enough for a couple of days, then we'll have to live off the land like Uncle Bert was going to.' He'd said it, quite naturally, without shuddering. In the excitement of planning, Uncle Bert had joined them, so casually that Sue hadn't even noticed.

'How? Catch things, you mean?'

'Y-e-s, that too. But I'm going to take the rifle with us as well. That should see us through.'

Privately, Sue felt a little doubtful about Jack's confidence. She didn't even know whether he knew how to fire a rifle, but perhaps he'd learned from some of the boys at school. A lot of them went out shooting with their fathers and brothers at week-ends. Sue shook her doubts away, and they went on with their choice—discussing, rejecting, accepting and rejecting again, until they had an assortment of gear and food that balanced between the minimum Jack wanted to carry, and the amount Sue felt was necessary.

In the end they decided to take the sultanas and an unopened packet of raisins, the bread (which, even though it was bulky was light), two tins of stew and one of beans, the can opener, one spoon, which they would share, the oranges and the billy. How to carry them was the next problem, which Jack solved by dumping the flour out in a great exploding white volcano, and using the bag.

'Right,' said Jack, when they were finished. 'The next step is to fill up the waterbag and let it soak a bit, and then fix up something for you to walk with.'

The waterbag was carefully filled, for even though they couldn't possibly take all the water in the drum, Jack still felt reluctant to waste a drop. The wire handle of the bag was hooked over a broken branch, and the bag hung there, its canvas turning slowly from dusty white to brown as the water oozed through in great glistening droplets, beading its swollen sides with the promise of coolness to come.

Finding makeshift crutches for Sue took Jack longer than he had anticipated. Tomahawk in hand he climbed out of the gully and roamed through the scrub. It was amazing how few suitable pieces of wood there were; they were all too short, too thick, too thin, or impossible to reach. Once he found a stick on the ground which was an ideal size, but when he tested it the wood was dead and rotten, and broke under his weight. A second stick, which he managed to chop off a tree, split along its length when he was almost through. Finally he had to make do with one crutch and one shorter stick. The crutch was pretty good, he thought, and even had a fork at the top for Sue's armpit. He left it fairly long so that he could cut it to the right size after Sue had tried it. The stick was merely a short dead branch, with a smooth round bulge at one end that had once been a gall, but had now weathered into a knob that just fitted his hand.

Jack returned triumphantly to the camp and, after measuring carefully, cut the crutch so that it would just fit comfortably. Sue tried walking with the combination crutch and stick, but after taking a few jerky hops she complained,

'It's awfully hard under my arm.'

'Can we wrap something round it?'

There was little in the way of spare clothing, but they tried using Sue's blouse and shorts. These kept slipping off. With a flash of inspiration, Jack remembered the blankets. He set to and, by using the tomahawk and a sadly blunted knife, eventually managed to hack off several long strips. He wound these round and round the top of the crutch until they made a fairly firm pad; then he took the two ends down and tied them in a bulky knot around the shaft of the crutch.

Sue tried again, and was pleased with the result. Now that she could rest more comfortably on the armpiece, she was able to develop quite a professional swing to her progress.

'That's terrific,' she said, 'let's go.'

'Hey, hang on a minute,' laughed Jack, 'we're not just strolling down to the corner. Besides, it's getting late.' He'd been conscious all the morning of the sun steadily working its way across the sky, until now it stood almost overhead.

'It must be nearly midday, so we'd be mad to set off now. We'd only get lost if we didn't know which way was west. I vote we cook a last really big feed, eat all we can, and then wait till the sun's moved on a bit so we know exactly where we're heading.'

'Suits me,' agreed Sue.

With Jack working, and Sue hopping about offering to help, but more often getting in his way, they built a small fire. Jack emptied a tin of stew and a tin of beans into the frying pan and, as a last grand fling, boiled up the billy and made tea. It was almost too hot to want food, but they managed to finish it all off, and lay back, replete and drowsy. With an effort, Jack rose and stamped out the fire. Before sitting down again he carefuly checked the remaining matches. There were fourteen. With a bit of luck they'd be rescued before they were all used up. They'd certainly need matches to cook the meat Jack was planning to shoot. Perhaps, once they reached the safety of the waterholes they could keep a small fire going all the time.

He sat down beside Sue, his back up against the gully wall, and almost instantly fell asleep. He awoke with a guilty start, and looked anxiously at the sky. The sun was about half-way down the sky, but there were still several hours of daylight. Enough for them to cover probably a couple of miles. Then camp for one night, and reach the hills easily tomorrow. He woke Sue, who had also fallen asleep, and they gathered up their loads. Jack topped up the waterbag until the water bubbled out of the china spout, and screwed the cap on tightly. At the last minute he dropped the three cans of beer into the flourbag with the rest of the food and the box of cartridges. He found he couldn't manage the billy, and was about to leave it behind when he thought of hooking its handle over the spout of the waterbag. Fortunately the rifle had a strap and he was able to sling it across his shoulder. With the flourbag across his other shoulder, and carrying the waterbag, he was ready. The waterbag was terribly heavy, and its wire handle cut into his fingers. Jack wished he had thought of padding it with strips of blanket too, but it was too late now for he didn't want to waste any more time.

He found, however, that he immediately had to unload again, as it was impossible to scramble out of the gully with all his gear on. In the end he had to make four trips up and down the gully walls: once with the food, once with the waterbag, once with the rifle and Sue's sticks and, finally, to help Sue.

As he loaded up again, Jack stood for a moment looking down at the litter of their camp. For a brief instant he wanted to dash down there again, unload his gear, and just wait, for the camp suddenly represented the security of his whole life. But he couldn't. Sue was already hobbling on ahead. Jack's eyes strayed down the gully to where he thought he could just make out a glimpse of the roof of the van. No, he thought, there's nothing down there now but death. Settling his shoulders more comfortably under their load Jack stooped, picked up the waterbag, and set off after Sue.

For the first quarter of a mile or so they made reasonable, if erratic, progress. Jack quickly took the lead, and concentrated on picking the easiest path through the scrub, trying to avoid projecting bushes or anything that would hinder Sue. Sue needed both hands to cope with her two sticks, and found she was unable to push aside the branches and twigs which scraped across her face and dragged at her hair. The homemade crutches were only moderately successful, for their splintery ends caused them to catch in the ground, so that she had to tug them free at almost every step. To make matters worse, neither of them had a free hand to cope with the flies, which clung with sticky tenacity around nose, mouth and eyes.

After a particularly tiring detour around a tangled clump of saltbush and scrub, Jack called a halt. His face was dripping with sweat, for there was not the slightest breath of air stirring to bring relief. Sue's hair, too, was plastered as wetly down her forehead as though she had been in swimming. She immediately collapsed on the ground with a sigh, and began to massage her armpit which was beginning to feel sore and numb from the pressure of the crutch. Unlike proper crutches, which have a crossbar where the hand can take some of the weight, Sue had to put her full pressure on the armpit at every step. In addition, she had to curl her hand sideways round the shaft of the stick, which was tiring and difficult, and already she had collected a few splinters, and the beginnings of a crop of blisters.

Jack set down the waterbag, and uncurled his fingers from around the handle. They were curved together like a claw, and he felt for a moment that he would never be able to straighten them out again. Swinging the flourbag from his shoulder, he used his right hand to straighten out the bent fingers, and then rubbed them hard, watching the skin redden as the blood flowed back. He flexed his hand violently open and shut several times: he couldn't remember anything as good as the relief of being able to stretch his fingers.

'How far do you think we've come?'

Jack squinted up his eyes while he tried to work it out. It was just a mile from home to school, and he tried to compare that walk with the length they had just travelled. It didn't seem quite as far, although it had taken a lot longer. With detours and so on, it was probably pretty much the same.

'I'm not sure. About a mile I reckon,' he finally decided. 'If we can get as far again before dark, we'll be nearly half-way there. Then we'll camp for the night and do the rest in easy stages tomorrow.'

Sue reached for her crutch and stick.

'We'd better get on then.'

Jack eyed her with concern. 'How's it going?'

'I'm okay,' Sue lied, 'you're the one that has to cart all that stuff.'

'Yeah!' Jack grimaced as he rearranged his load, shifting the waterbag and the flourbag to opposite hands. The worst thing of all was the rifle. Made for a burly adult shoulder, the strap was far too long for Jack's thin frame, and the rifle continually slipped off balance, swinging wildly, catching in everything, and bashing against his hip. But he would not leave it behind.

He dare not leave it behind. It was his symbol of survival. With it, he could take on his man's rôle in this world where only a man could survive. The rifle was food, courage, security; it was proof against death by starvation; it was the calm competent self-assurance of bluff friendly Uncle Bert, now rotting in his four-wheeled grave. It was also his enemy, a useless tool he didn't even know how to fire; a vicious *thing* that impeded his progress, but also something on which Jack could centre his anger and frustration. It was only anger and frustration that prevented him from giving in to the icy hopelessness of his and Sue's insane journey. A frightened boy, and a frightened crippled girl, trudging towards nowhere—two forlorn specks of nothing on the face of this alien, hostile land.

Nothing going straight to nowhere!

He glanced towards Sue. She was standing, propped up, waiting for him to lead off. He had to admit that she didn't look frightened. Well, he was frightened. He switched the rifle angrily into position, grabbed up his two loads, and started off again.

Carefully he kept their faces always towards the sun, which was now disappearing behind the trees in front of them as they struggled on. Rests became more and more frequent, but Jack was determined to keep going as long as the sun was up. Even when they didn't actually rest, Jack had to pause often to change hands. He felt after a while that his arms were being stretched out of their sockets, and he imagined the bones of his elbows and shoulders slowly parting company. Much more of this, and my knuckles'll be trailing on the ground like a gorilla's, he thought sourly. Still, it would be good for his monkey act!

'Don't be such a jackanapes!' Mr Foster had yelled at him one day, when Jack had asked a particularly idiotic question in class. At least, Jack hadn't thought the question was stupid until old Foster had jumped on him. Jack had gone hot with embarrassment as the class had burst into laughter, and later, in the playground, a group of boys had gathered around him taunting, 'Jackanapes! Jackanapes!' So Jack had picked on the only part of the word he understood—'apes'—and started bouncing up and down, knees bent, arms doubled up to scratch at his ribs, and grunting like a chimpanzee. Like his drunk act, this had turned their laughter for him instead of against him. Since then, a cry of jackanapes, or Jack the Ape, always brought forth the teasers and onlookers. In time the word was no longer used to tease, but was accepted by Jack as a title honouring his performance.

His mind jumped back to the present.

Now all he could think about was stopping. Only the belief that soon they would be nearly half-way there kept him plodding on. Tomorrow he didn't even think about.

From behind him there was a grunt and then a cry, and he turned to see Sue lying full length on the ground. Tears spilled from her eyes as she rolled over and tried to brush the dirt off her frock and knees.

'Can't we stop now, Jack?' she pleaded. 'We must have gone for miles.'

Jack gazed through the sparse bush ahead of them. There was still a glint of sunlight on the leaves, but already the sun was starting to sink below the horizon. By the time they had rested and loaded up again, it would be almost gone, and then they couldn't move anyway. As it was, it was becoming more and more difficult to be sure of heading in the right direction now that the sun was no longer directly on their faces but diffused by the scrub. More than anything else, Jack was terrified of becoming lost.

'Righto,' he said with relief, and dumped his equipment on to the ground.

He looked around. The area where they had stopped could hardly have been less like a camp. It was barely even a clearing, with scruffy mulga and saltbush all around. As soon as they stopped the flies zeroed in with increased persistence. Jack broke off a couple of leafy switches, handed one to Sue, and they flapped them with tired concentration.

With an effort Jack forced himself to his feet and started to potter around. He hung the waterbag from a branch, noticing with a worried frown that it had already left a damp patch on the ground. He felt the bag carefully, but it still seemed almost full. The lid of the billy had fallen off somewhere along the way, but that didn't matter too much.

'Can we have a drink now?' asked Sue. Jack had refused to broach the waterbag at any of their previous halts. What we should have done, he thought ruefully, was to have drunk all the water we could hold before we left. Maybe we could've stored it up like camels!

He dug the one mug out of the flourbag and filled it up for Sue, who gulped it down without stopping.

'Ah,' she breathed, 'that was lovely.'

Jack refilled the mug and drank his share. He tried to drink it slowly to savour it, but found his throat was forcing him to gulp it down too. It was cool, with a faintly dusty canvas taste, but it brought wonderful relief. With regret Jack screwed the top back on the bag and upended the mug over the spout. How lovely it would be to go on and on drinking, but they dare not.

Having learnt from the previous night's experience, Jack was determined to keep their food safe from likely scavengers. He tried hanging it up, but this proved impossible, as there was no way to tie it on. Eventually Jack managed to poke a hole through the neck of the bag and spear it on to a broken, sharp bough. It didn't look too safe, but it was the best he could manage. At least it would be reasonably safe from pests.

'No fire tonight, Sue,' he said when he had finished. 'We're too close to the scrub. It isn't safe.'

'What about snakes?'

'Oh, we'll be all right. We haven't seen a single snake so far, so I don't think they'll trouble us.'

'But – ' Surely snakes sought out the warmth of human bodies, and you woke up with a poisonous tiger snake curled up on your chest. Sue shuddered. It had been different when they had had a fire going, but looking at Jack she realized there was no point in arguing with him. Besides, even snakes would be better than a bushfire, and Jack was right, there really was nowhere safe to set a fire. As if to confirm her thoughts, a light wind sprang up and strengthened rapidly, sending dead leaves and dust skirling across the ground.

'I think,' continued Jack, pursuing his own line of thought, 'we ought to go to sleep as soon as we can, and get a really early start in the morning. We'll save our big meal up for breakfast so we can have plenty to travel on, and polish off some bread and raisins for tea.'

Sue nodded in agreement. She was almost too tired to care, and she wasn't really hungry. It was still too hot.

Jack unhooked the flourbag and dug out the bread. Even inside its greaseproof wrapping, the bread had dried out, and each slice was twisted into weird curves like dry leaves. It tasted incredibly gritty by itself, and they found that they swallowed each mouthful in a gluey lump which seemed to stick half-way down their gullets. A few squashy raisins completed the main meal, and they finished with an orange each. Jack had hoped that the oranges would stop them wanting any more to drink, but they turned out to be mostly pulp and skin, with very little juice. Reluctantly, Jack refilled the mug with water, and they drank half each.

Then, smoothing the soil as best they could, they both settled down for the night. The dusk deepened into darkness, and they slept fitfully, aware of their own discomfort, of vague scurryings and scuttlings and sudden cries in the bush around them, and of the increasing blustering of the wind.

They had travelled just over one mile . . .

CHAPTER SIX

They awoke again next morning at first light, and Jack set about preparing a quick but substantial breakfast of cold stew and beans mixed together. To his surprise, it turned out to be quite tasty and very satisfying. They each washed it down with a long swig of water, but Jack saw, with dismay, that the waterbag was only about two-thirds full. Still, they should make the hills easily by midday.

The strong breeze of the night before had turned into a full-blown gale, hurtling straight from the west, and bearing with it the savage heat and debris of half a continent. The trees, normally limp and still, were grabbed and twisted and torn as the wind blundered past. The leaves which should have shone and glistened in the early morning sunlight wore a dull layer of dust from the inland. Already the temperature was in the nineties, and by noon it would be well over one hundred degrees. As Jack stood up again, the wind savaged and jostled him, and flying grit and sand forced him to narrow his eyes to a slit. The blast seemed to suck every drop of moisture out of his body as it swept by. Jack licked his lips with a tongue that already was like a dry and dusty piece of calico. He frowned. They would be walking directly into the wind until they reached the shelter of the hills!

Sue was busy adjusting her crutches, and winding the grubby handkerchief around her hand where a couple of blisters had rubbed raw.

As a final check, Jack clambered up a small tree and peered westwards towards the hills.

'Oh, God,' he groaned. 'It's not possible. We must have come farther than that.'

The hills seemed as tantalizingly far away as when he had sighted them before they left the gully. He was positive they had kept heading in the right direction yesterday. There had been no big detours, and even when they had been forced to turn aside to circle a clump of bush, he had always got straight back into line again. Anxiously he checked the sun. Yes, it was directly behind him, shining straight at the hills.

He and Sue felt fresh enough now, but yesterday had proved they couldn't travel on for too long. He was prepared to cover the same distance, but more than that? He didn't know. And what about Sue? How long could he keep on encouraging her? Perhaps, he thought desperately, it's the dust haze that makes the hills seem so far away. He tried to convince himself of the truth of this, but although he yearned to take comfort from the thought, his mind refused to be fooled. The hills were still miles and miles away; they would have to travel at least twice as far as they had already.

Sick at heart, his stomach churning over, he slid down the tree, and busied himself with his gear, keeping his eyes averted from Sue. He knew that if he looked at her she must read the truth there, and he was afraid.

'You ready?' Still not looking at her.

'Just about. How much farther is it?'

Jack wanted to ignore the question, but he couldn't. Trying to keep his voice casual, he replied, 'It's a bit hard to tell with the dust everywhere. About as far as yesterday, perhaps a little bit more.' His voice sounded dry and constricted, and he was aware of Sue glancing at him.

'This damn' dust!' he swore, and made a great show of clearing his throat, coughing and spitting. Sue frowned. There was something wrong.

'We're not lost, are we? We are on the right track?' Her fear blurted it out.

'Of course we're not lost. Don't be so stupid,' Jack snapped, glad to be able to work off some of his own fear in irritation. 'How on earth could we be lost? We've been heading due west all the time. The hills are due west,' he gestured, 'straight over there. I've just been up to check, and they're there, I saw them.'

'All right, don't get so mad. I was only asking.'

'I'm sorry.' Jack forced himself to look at Sue, a direct and candid glance. He must convince her that everything was in order, or they would both be lost. He knew now that he had strength enough to live with his own fear, but he could not control Sue's fears too. His . . . their only chance was to force her to believe what he said.

'I said I was sorry,' he repeated. 'It's just that we're both tired and frightened, and then this wind. It really gets my goat.' He smiled, and Sue smiled back, though Jack was sure Sue would know he was only baring his teeth against taut lips. But Sue didn't seem to notice.

Jack helped her to her feet, saw her settled, shouldered his own load, and turned into the wind.

It was much harder to be sure of their direction travelling with the sun behind him, as the load he was carrying prevented him from feeling the sun evenly on his back. While the sun was still low in the east the shadows from the scrub helped, but as the sun rose higher, the shadows grew shorter. There was a patch of thicker scrub here, and it was difficult to pick out individual shadows, even his own diminishing one stumping along ahead of him.

Their progress was painfully slow and uneven, and as their first freshness wore off, muscles, bruises and blisters already battered the day before, began to protest. To stop himself from thinking about his aching body, Jack tried to concentrate on distance, and work out their trek logically. If it's six miles, he thought, how many feet is that? He couldn't remember the number of feet in a mile, but it was 1760 yards, he thought. That's 1760 multiplied by three and then by six, which is . . . nought, eight, two—5280 times six. He couldn't concentrate sufficiently, and tried another approach. He watched his trudging feet, trying to estimate the distance he covered at each step. Perhaps nearly a foot, more if he included his own foot length as well. Let's say, then, that it takes six thousand steps to walk one mile.

If it's six miles, that'll be 36,000 steps. How fast can someone walk—three miles an hour, wasn't it? But that would be ordinary walking on a footpath. We're going through rough bush, with detours and all. Suppose I'm walking two miles an hour—but then I have to keep stopping to let Sue catch up. Okay, I'll make it one mile an hour. That's six hours! Then, of course, we have to rest, and we can't go on while the sun's right overhead. Yes, we can, we can keep facing into the wind. Suppose the wind changes? No, we'll have to stop for a couple of hours.

If we cover one thousand feet and then have a rest, that's thirty-six rests. If each rest is fifteen minutes, that's . . . let's see. There are four fifteens in an hour, so that's thirty-six divided by four, which is nine hours! That's ridiculous! The whole day will be gone just in resting. We'll have to do at least two thousand steps before we rest. That means four and a half hours spent in rests, and six hours in walking. Crikey! Even then we might not make it by tonight.

Jack's mind shrank from the possibility, and he started counting paces, concentrating his whole mind on the simple repetitive numbers. He could hear Sue thumping and stumbling along behind him, occasionally giving a small cry as a branch or twig scraped and scratched her. His only consolation, he realized, was that the waterbag was lighter today, and that was hardly cause for rejoicing.

They travelled, and rested, and took mouthfuls of water that only served to make them more conscious of their thirst, and their parched bodies. With a part of his mind Jack hated Sue, and the wind, and the bush, and Uncle Bert: everything that had conspired to get him into this fix. If only he could suddenly drop all his gear, grab the precious waterbag, and run and run and run until his lungs were bursting. Run until he reached the hills and their water. He pictured Sue trying to run after him, tripping, falling, her voice shrieking with fear as he left her far, far behind. He dwelt on her fear, almost with relish, and it lessened his own. To know that he had the power to reduce her to cowering terror at any moment gave him added strength. While his body trudged so slowly and painfully through the dust and unendurable heat, his imagination ran riot. Sometimes he saw himself standing over Sue, taunting her brutally, and laughing fiendishly as he drank the last of their water. At other times he imagined a cool shaded rock pool into which he plunged, down and down and down, to float endlessly in its wet dim depths. Like a fish flicking through the water, not even needing to breathe, his body lapped forever in liquid softness.

So they plodded on, and rested; on, and rested, each only partly aware of the presence of the other. The sun climbed high in the sky, and they flopped, benumbed, in the sand. There was no proper rest, even now, when they did not need to force their protesting bodies on again for several hours. The sun beat down; the wind whipped stinging particles against their exposed skin. Jack's shoulder was rubbed raw from the rifle strap, and Sue's hands were bleeding from blisters and splinters. Even though they were brown, the sun had burned their faces and the backs of their necks. Worst of all, the waterbag was now almost empty, and it both taunted and threatened them with its dwindling supply.

Jack had refused to let either of them have another drink until they could actually see the hills. Sue, after a brief grumble, agreed, for she too realized by now that perhaps they might not reach their destination that day. Instead, they shared the last orange for lunch, since neither of them had any stomach for food, but its withered quarters did little to relieve their thirst. Then they sat, slumped and motionless, while the wind swept over and past them. The air was scorching hot, and the bush, apart from the rattle of leaves and the drone of the wind, was as quiet as though every other living thing had died.

When the sun had passed its peak and once again led them to the west, they stood up and went on. There were no thoughts now, just endless, mechanical movement. Even if he wanted to, Jack no longer had the strength to run, and the waterbag was no longer worth stealing. The world was a huge, blazing treadmill. They had been walking like this forever, and there was no end to it.

Never an end . . .

After a while they came to the edge of the scrub and stood facing an almost bare patch of gibber plain. There at last they could see the hills, shimmering in the heat haze, and dark against the declining sun. Great lakes of silver water lapped the base of each hill, but Jack and Sue knew it was only a mirage. The hills rose harsh and stony from the bare dusty plain. Jack guessed they were probably still a couple of miles away, but at least now they could see their goal.

Away from the scrub that held them back, and with the end in sight, they should have plunged forward with renewed enthusiasm, but it was too late for that. Jack still doubted if they would reach the hills by nightfall, and Sue was afraid they would never reach them at all. Perhaps next time she looked up they would have vanished like the pools of water that shrank and shrivelled the nearer you came, until suddenly they were no longer there and you didn't even know where they had been.

Irrelevantly, Sue remembered a film she had seen with a diving scene in it, in which it had been made to look as though the divers were falling upwards out of the water and back on to the diving board. She remembered how funny it had been, and how they had laughed as all the water, down to the last little splash, had been sucked backwards until the surface of the pool was flat and smooth. That's how mirages were. As though a giant, or more likely a bunyip, lay just beneath the ground and sucked them away with a silent swoosh so that they drained out of sight. Sue watched the diving scene, which seemed to be projected on to a screen inside her head, and chuckled happily. Already she was half delirious.

The gibber plain proved even harder to travel over than the scrub. The stones shifted and twisted under Sue's sticks, and often she almost lost her balance and fell. The sun, directly ahead of them, flamed relentlessly, and the light, reflected back off the stones, hurt their eyes, so that they could barely keep them open. Without the slight protection of the straggly scrub, the sun scorched their reddened skin, until Jack thought that walking through a burning house could hardly have been more painful.

Mouths cracked and parched, each breath searing their lungs, they staggered on, not aware of any individual pain, only of a huge agony that engulfed their whole bodies. The wind whipped grit into their eyes, ears, noses and mouths, until it seemed likely that they would turn into part of the desert itself. Jack tried to imagine lying under a giant waterfall, mouth gaping, and letting tons and tons of water flood into him until he was as swollen and bloated as a water-filled balloon. But he found it hard to concentrate on anything for long, and the dream only made him feel worse.

He had lost count of the number of times they stopped, collapsing on to the baking earth. Each stop was longer than the last, but brought no rest to aching muscles and tortured bodies; and each time it was that much harder to get up and go on.

Towards sunset they drank the last of the water from the shrunken waterbag. There was barely a cupful each and it was lukewarm. It tasted thick on their coated tongues, like drinking liquid dust, and only seemed to make their thirst worse.

Jack rubbed his hands despairingly over his face. The hills were closer now, barely half a mile away, and silhouetted starkly black against the crimson sky. It must have taken them about four hours to do the last stretch, and Jack knew they'd never make the rest before darkness fell. Even if they did, there'd be no time to climb the hills and find the waterholes. If they existed! They must exist, he cried silently, nodding his head to convince himself. If only he wasn't burdened by Sue, he could hurry on, find water, fill the waterbag, and return to her before night.

'Can you make it any farther?'

Sue shook her head dumbly. Grimy, sunburnt, sweat-streaked, her face drawn with weariness and pain, she looked nothing like a child, rather some ageless incarnation of the desert.

'Sue? Could you stay here with the things? I'll try and get to the hills for water and come back again.'

Fear sparked in her eyes.

'No!' Her lips moved, but no sound came out. She swallowed convulsively and tried again.

'No!' It was a harsh, dry croak, as though the day of silent struggle had made her forget how to talk. 'Don't leave me. You'll get lost. You'll never find me again!'

Jack heard the undertone of hysterical terror in her voice.

'I couldn't posibly lose you,' he tried to joke, 'you stick out here like a bump on a log.'

There was no answering smile from Sue, who stared at him hopelessly. If he decided to go, she would die. Just twitch and frizzle up like a spider on a burning log. She wanted to tell Jack that only his dogged determination had kept her going all day, and the belief that together they would survive. But her brain was pounded into numbness by the heat and the suffocating, endless wind, and she couldn't think. She just shook her head again helplessly, and whispered, 'Don't go.'

Jack tried to grin reassuringly.

'Okay,' he said. 'Whatever you say. Anyway, we'll be fresher in the morning, and make it easily. It's not far now, and once we reach the water our troubles'll be over.' He tried to make it sound convincing, but he doubted if Sue was even listening. Secretly he was relieved that he didn't have to travel any farther. Even if he reached the hills, he'd still have to find the waterholes. He was pretty sure he'd never be able to carry a full waterbag back across the plain either, even if he could beat the darkness.

A flock of parrots flew shrieking overhead, and were soon lost as they swooped into the shadow of the hills.

There must be water there if the birds are heading that way, Jack told himself. There *must*.

Sue lay slumped on the ground, apparently unaware of any discomfort from rocks and stones. Jack got the water-bag, wrapped it over a largish flat stone, and pushed it over to Sue.

'Here, put your head on this.'

Sue looked up at him dully, but obediently lifted her head, and Jack manœuvred the stone into position. Sue turned on to her side, back to the wind, and curled up almost into a ball. Jack stood up, staggering slightly, and moved off a few paces to relieve himself.

As he watched the thin stream disappear into the earth, he suddenly thought of the stories some of the kids at school used to tell. Cec King said you went mad if you drank your own water. But Bluey Scott's father had been a soldier in New Guinea, and Bluey said his father swore by it as a cure for trench foot. Ron Sawtell claimed the Blacks always drank their pee, and there were many other stories whispered and giggled over behind the school lavatories. With an effort Jack forced himself to stop in midstream and, fly still unzippered, got the mug. By the time he had finished peeing it was almost full. He carried it carefully back, zipped up his jeans, and sat down. He stared at the mug. It was still hot from his body, and he picked it up again tentatively. He craved for fluid, any fluid, even this, but his stomach rebelled. He raised the mug closer, and sniffed cautiously. There was very little smell, which surprised him. He brought the mug almost up to his lips, then, with a sudden gesture of disgust, turned and poured it on to the ground, where it soaked in almost without trace. Immediately he regretted the impulse, and flung the mug clattering on to the stones.

'Damn! Damn! Damn!' he swore. He wanted to cry from tiredness and anger and the heavy load of responsibility he had carried all day, but there were no tears left to come. The sun had scorched them all away.

He grabbed the flour sack and shoved it roughly into

position, then flopped down full length. His head hit the sack harder than he had intended, and he swore again. Sitting up, he savagely rummaged through the bag, emptying its contents on to the ground. It was then that he found the cans of beer, which he had completely forgotten.

'I'll save them till the morning,' he said, taking a sudden self-sacrificing pleasure in the thought. His body had betrayed him, had made him suffer all through the terrible day's journey, and now he would punish it by refusing it comfort. Besides, there was Sue to consider. They'd share the beer at breakfast, and it would be enough to keep them going until they found water.

Rolling the empty sack into a thin, unsatisfactory pillow, he lay back. The red had already faded from the sky, and the first faint stars were visible. 'I never want to move again,' thought Jack. His eyelids drooped, and within minutes he had joined Sue in a sleep of utter exhaustion.

CHAPTER SEVEN

Jack awoke to the harsh screams of a flock of birds which were brawling and bickering amongst themselves as they pecked for food around the sparse bushes in the gibbers. He sat up immediately, and felt quite light-headed. Sue was still asleep, but he shook her awake.

'Come on,' he said, 'last leg of the trip.'

Sue looked at him uncomprehendingly, and hardly seemed aware of where they were, but she too sat up. Jack piled the remaining food and their few bits of equipment into the flourbag. His head was swimming, and he knew they probably both needed something to eat, but he was no longer hungry. All he wanted was to reach the hills.

His mouth was lined with felt: he must have a drink! With a flourish he snapped the top off the first can of beer and foamed it out into the mug. It was warm, bitter, and mostly froth, but he forced it down. He found the second mugful poured out better if he ran the beer down the inside of the mug. He handed it to Sue.

She shook her head, but he insisted. Between them they drank two of the cans, and Jack stowed the third away for an emergency. Then, for the last time they set out.

Jack experienced an almost irresistible desire to run, laugh and shout, and he realized that he must be a little drunk. Sue, too, was reeling slightly, but despite this they were making better time than yesterday. Jack's body seemed strangely detached from the rest of him, and he was no longer so aware of discomfort. That must have been why they used to give people a drink of whisky before pulling out a tooth in the old days, he thought. He only wished they'd had its anaesthetic effect the day before.

Now the only thing that mattered was the hill. Mind, muscle, sinew and bone all strained after that one goal.

Although the change was imperceptible, it *must* be coming closer with every step. Floating outside himself, Jack was aware of his and Sue's slow, halting, dogged progress as they stumbled across the plain. At last, after an eternity, they collapsed, too spent for pain, or even the relief of stopping. They were at the base of the first hill.

It may have been ten minutes or ten hours that Jack and Sue lay sprawled in the dust. At last Jack became aware of the discomfort of various sharp stones sticking into him, and he stood up reluctantly, groaning slightly. The hill they had reached was the largest of the three, and rose steeply, straight out of the plain. The other two hills were smaller and lower, and ran back in a line to the left of the main one. Jack stared up the slope. Stunted shrubs grew here and there, leaning out from the rocky face at unlikely angles. About two-thirds of the way up he could just make out a clump of larger, denser scrub.

'If there *is* water, it must be up there,' Jack said, unaware that he was speaking out loud. Sue raised her head and looked at him, but his words didn't seem to register.

Jack studied the slope, trying to work out the easiest route up. Most of the surface was of worn rock, reminding Jack of a series of roofing tiles laid side by side, or of the overlapping scales of a shingle back lizard. Just to their right was a smooth, curved channel running straight up like a gutter.

Dumping his gear in a heap, Jack leaned over and shook Sue's shoulder.

'Sue, Sue! I'm going up to find the waterhole. You wait here. I won't be long.'

Sue stared at him.

'Sue!' He shook her more urgently. 'I've got to go and look for water, but I won't be long. Do you understand? Will you be all right here?'

Sue nodded slowly, and slumped down again.

Jack looked at her, frowning. He hated to leave her, but he couldn't do anything by staying. Only water, rest, and food would help now, and the longer he delayed, the worse it would be. With an impatient shake he forced himself to turn away and start the possibly fruitless climb. Behind him, totally forgotten in his exhaustion, the empty desiccated waterbag merged into the dust.

At first he headed straight up the gutter, but it was so smoothly polished by long vanished rains that he kept slipping. After skidding twice and barking his knuckles he moved on to the rocky hillside. Here the going was slightly easier, if somewhat rougher, and he had to concentrate on every step. The surface, close up, was a mosaic of projecting, oddly-shaped stone, each piece divided from the rest by large cracks and depressions which had worn away at a faster rate. Jack found that unless he stepped squarely in the centre of each raised piece, it was liable to crumble at the edge and send his foot thumping into one of the cracks with the awful risk of spraining his ankle.

The heat billowed up from the red-brown surface of the rocks, but fortunately the wind had dropped to an intermittent breeze. The air pulsated and pressed in on him, until Jack felt he was being squashed between a circle of inflating inner tubes. It was difficult to walk upright at times, but after one brief attempt at using his hands to help pull himself up Jack found that he had almost burned them on the scorching rocks. His thighs and calves were aching with the unaccustomed climbing. From time to time he was forced to stop. Already he was well above the plain, and Sue was no longer visible due to the slope of the hill. Feeling that the gutter was the best lead, he tried to follow its course. Now, as he stood to rest his rasping lungs, he saw that the gutter turned abruptly right, and then petered out between two large rocky boulders.

Jack felt his eyes prickle with tears of misery and defeat. There wasn't any water, after all. There wasn't any anything, only sand and rock and sun and heat and death. Uncle Bert had been wrong. It was all his uncle's fault, and he was glad, savagely and viciously glad, that Bert was dead. It served him right. At that moment Jack hated his uncle with all the bitterness and agony that had been building up inside him for the last few cruel days. He wanted to scream and kick and beat his head against those rocks; against the blindly vindictive fate that had led them here . . . to nothing.

Stooping, he grabbed a large stone and flung it with all his strength at the rocky, unyielding enemy. Blinded by rage, his shot went wide, and disappeared through the cleft in the rocks. Dimly he heard it clatter and plop . . .

Plop!

His anger drained away, and he stood for a minute, frozen and shivering with disbelief in the scorching sun. His legs were weak and trembling, and when he tried to go forwards they refused, at first, to obey him. Then slowly, step by step, he edged between the rocks. It wasn't true. It was only a trick to make him suffer more. It was . . . *water*.

Jack came through the passage and stood, his eyes riveted on the unbelievable sight. Here, in a depression between the boulders was a pool, dark, still and deep. As though it were a computer, his brain registered every detail of the scene. To his right stood an overhang of rock, almost forty feet long, still in shadow but high enough to stand up in. Directly in front of him was the pool. Beyond it a smooth cleft in the rock led, in a series of polished steps, to what seemed to be yet another pool above. On the left a patch of soil and scrub dwindled out to the bare, rocky shingles again. But even as he saw these scenes, Jack's eyes returned again and again to the pool.

With a wild meaningless yell he leaped forward, and half dived, half jumped into the water. A cluster of ducks which had been huddling together at the far end of the pool and eyeing him suspiciously, took to the air with a clatter of wings and affronted honkings and squawkings. Jack didn't even hear them. He was paddling and turning and diving, his head beneath the water, and gulping down great choking mouthfuls. It was pure and sweet and cool, but Jack wouldn't have cared if it had tasted like diesel oil!

At last, gasping and panting he rested, treading water. When he had got his breath back he turned and slowly swam to the far end and back again. He would spend the rest of his life here, just floating and swimming and drinking. He took another few mouthfuls, more slowly this time. He rolled them round and round his mouth to rinse it, then spurted the water out in a great spluttering jet. Grinning, he ducked his head beneath the surface, opened his eyes, blew bubbles, spurted and kicked, and splashed in ecstasy.

Tiring at last, and hampered by his sodden clothes and boots, he tried to touch bottom, but the sides of the pool seemed to dip straight down. In a few strokes, he reached the edge, and hauled himself out, panting. Even the sun felt good now.

With a shock he remembered Sue.

He turned and ran, enjoying the flapping of his wet jeans and the squelching of his boots. By the time he reached the foot of the hill they were almost dry.

Sue was lying huddled up in the same position he had left her. Her mouth was half open, and she was breathing in quick shallow gasps. Jack was appalled when he saw her, and cursed himself for forgetting her in his own wild excitement. At his urging Sue stood up, but swayed and nearly fell again. She seemed dazed and unaware of where she was or what was happening. Even if she'd been well and strong, Jack knew she would never make it up the hill with her two cumbersome crutches.

He bent down in front of her.

'Here, Sue, climb on and I'll give you a piggy-back up.'

Jack helped her curl her legs round his waist. As he tried to straighten up, he found Sue didn't even have enough strength to hold on to his shoulders. Terrified that she would fall off, Jack knelt down again quickly and wriggled her off. She sat, a floppy doll, where he had put her.

'Oh, God,' he thought, 'please don't let her die.'

Together they could survive, but not alone. Not alone.

Somehow he must carry Sue up there. He must. Again he helped her to stand, then he bent and angled her over one shoulder so that her head hung down his back. Although she was so skinny, Jack found that her dead weight was more than he had expected; and in her half-conscious state she was hard to hold. Gritting his teeth, and staggering slightly off balance, Jack started the long climb up again.

He never knew how he managed to make it. Towards the end he was moving like a mindless zombie, only the thought of water for Sue driving him on and on. At times he even began to doubt what he had seen. Perhaps there never had been a pool. Perhaps this was just some endless nightmare through which he staggered on and on. But at last he came to the passage through the rocks and out to the pool.

The ducks, which had returned by now, didn't bother to wait for another disturbance, but flew off at once, protesting raucously.

Panting and gasping, Jack shuffled Sue down. Pulling off his boots, he dangled his feet in the water for a few minutes while he caught his breath. Sue lay face up to the sun, her eyelids slightly parted. Rapidly Jack began to splash her face and body with water. If only the pool hadn't been so deep he would have pulled her right in and supported her himself; but he wasn't a good enough swimmer to hold Sue up and swim as well.

Gradually Sue began to stir. Jack realized with annoyance that he had forgotten to bring up a mug for her to drink out of. Sprinkling was too slow, so, picking up one of his boots, Jack used it to pour a steady stream of water over her head and neck. At last Sue opened her eyes. Filling his boot again, Jack held it to her lips. Sue seemed unaware of the strange cup, for after a few hesitant sips she gulped greedily. Jack refilled it again, and eventually she drank three bootfuls, spilling some of it in her eagerness.

Already she looked better, and her breathing was more regular. When he was sure she had drunk all she wanted, Jack poured more water over her until her frock was soaked and clinging wet. Then, with an effort, he helped her over to the overhang. It could hardly be called a cave, but at least it offered some protection from the sun. With a sigh,

Sue settled on to the shady sand, and almost instantly fell asleep.

As soon as he saw Sue was all right, Jack turned once more and trekked down the hill for the last time. He had to salvage the rest of their gear; but now he could take it more slowly. Fortunately, since they had eaten or drunk most of their provisions, the load wasn't too heavy. Although the rifle and Sue's two sticks were awkward to carry, Jack managed to bring the lot up in one trip.

When he got back, Sue was still asleep, so Jack dumped everything down and stretched out beside her. He was completely knocked up.

They might well be here for a long, long time, and he would have to plan things carefully from now on. But there would be plenty of time for that, he thought drowsily. First he must rest. Even as he thought, he fell asleep and the ducks, which had been watching from farther up the hill, flew back and settled, unmolested, in their pool.

When Jack next opened his eyes, he had no idea of the time or even what day it was. He guessed it was morning from the position of the sun, but which morning he didn't know. He rolled over to look at Sue, grimacing as aching muscles and shoulders reminded him painfully of yesterday's labours.

Sue was lying on her back, her eyes open. As he stirred, she shifted to look at him. Jack was relieved to see that she seemed to be herself again today.

'Where are we?' she asked.

'At the waterholes—at last.'

'Truly?'

'Sure. Don't you remember?'

'Unh-unh.' Sue shook her head. 'Only walking and walking and walking.'

It was wonderful to have someone to talk to again, and to be relieved of the lonely pressure and worry of travelling on, of having to supply the will and strength for two. Jack found the words bubbling out as he described the events of the day before, joking about it and clowning it up in his relief. He described the pool, and even giving Sue a drink out of his boot.

'Erk,' she said, pulling a face, but she smiled, too, for the first time for days.

'I don't remember a thing about getting here,' she repeated with a puzzled frown when Jack had finished his saga. 'All that climbing right up here.'

Jack reddened. He hadn't told Sue that he had actually carried her on his back. Suddenly it seemed embarrassing, like all those phony heroes Mrs Barker used to tell them about: the boy on the burning deck (the great dope, sitting there waiting to die just because no one had told him to leave his post), and that Dutch boy with his finger in the dike, and Grace Darling. There was something unreal about heroics like that. Jack knew he was no hero, and he was ashamed of admitting to his deed. He'd be like all the rest of those tinpot creeps, skiting about what he'd done, yet pretending it was nothing, and all the while lapping up the praise and the glory. He'd only carried Sue because there was no other choice. If he was going to be the centre of attention, it would only be because he chose to be, by acting the ox. No one was going to make a goody-goody hero out of him, not even Sue.

'Just let's say you made it,' he laughed.

But Sue kept on worrying at the problem. Jack had vividly described the hill to her, and she found it impossible to imagine covering such territory without any recollection of it.

'Well,' grinned Jack at last, 'if you really want to know, a big fat emu came along and offered you a lift. So I hoisted you on to his back, and you rode up here in style, just like Lady Muck.'

'No, don't be an idiot,' persisted Sue, but Jack stuck to his story and, half laughing, half crossly, Sue finally gave in. To change the subject, she added, 'Did you look at the roof of the cave?'

'No. Why?' Jack gazed above him. The sandstone overhang was in shadow, but he thought he could see markings on it.

'You'll have to stand up to see it properly now,' said Sue, 'but the sun was on it earlier, and it's all covered with drawings.'

Jack creaked to his feet. Standing upright, the roof was only a few inches above his head, and now he could make out all sorts of marks. There were dozens of handprints, outlined in red; apparently meaningless patterns of white spots; several lizard- or goanna-like creatures; and, winding between them all, a twisty snake in bands of red. white and yellow ochre. Jack traced it along with his finger, and it ran the whole length of the roof. It would have been thirty or forty feet long.

'This must have been an Abos' camp,' said Sue when Jack had finished. She was now sitting up and watching him.

'Yeah. Maybe a sacred hunting ground sort of place.'

'Perhaps it still is.'

'I dunno. These are pretty faint now.'

'But it might still be used,' persisted Sue. 'If it is, then someone will come out here and find *us*.'

Jack looked sharply at Sue. Although she seemed better, he realized she was still afraid. He was too, he admitted to himself. The worst part was over, he knew, and now that they had a permanent water supply they would be able to survive, but for how long he didn't know. It would depend on his hunting abilities. Even if these were first rate, which he doubted, they wouldn't want to stay here forever.

'You may be right,' he said, partly to dispel Sue's worries, and partly to banish his own uncertainty. 'I know some of the old blokes in town still follow the tribal customs, and go walkabout and all that.'

'Well, they'd be bound to come up here to hunt, wouldn't they?' asked Sue. 'After all, there's water and everything here.'

The thought of food reminded Jack that he was ravenous. His stomach started to rumble in hollow sympathy.

'How about some tucker?'

'Ooh, yes,' agreed Sue.

Jack opened the final tin of stew. Better to start out feeling full instead of saving it up and doling out a little bit at a time. There were still a few slices of bread from their last loaf. They were as dry as cement, so Jack broke them up and stirred them into the stew. To finish up they divided the rest of the crunchy, sugary clump of sultanas—about a handful each.

'There's still one can of beer left. Will I open it?' he asked.

'No, just water.'

Jack soaked the waterbag in the pool. Then he held it under the surface to fill it until the last bubble had gurgled out, and carried it back to the cave.

Jack decided that whoever had done the drawings would have chosen a spot that was protected from all but the very worst weather, otherwise the drawings would have been worn away almost as quickly as they were done. They would have been blasted away by the gritty winds, faded by the sun, or washed off by the rains which, when they did eventually come, were usually regular cloudbursts. The opening of the overhang must therefore face roughly north to east, away from prevailing weather, he reckoned, so it would do just fine for them.

It was wonderful to have all the water they needed. They drank two mugfuls down at once, still feeling they could never make up for the days of thirst. Jack trickled some over his head and tousled his hair until it stood up in spikes, and Sue complained that he was soaking the floor. In turn each took the mug and sat there, gazing at the pool and sipping the water. Sometimes they swilled it around their mouths, then squirted it out, just for the sheer joy of having enough to waste. Then they had a competition to see who could squirt it the farthest. Jack won, but only because, Sue complained, he cheated by leaning forwards. She even tried cleaning her teeth with her finger, but it didn't make much difference. This was a chore she'd always avoided whenever she could, but now she longed for a brush and some toothpaste: anything to get rid of the furry film of moss growing on her teeth.

Fed, relaxed, and happy, Jack felt confidence flowing back.

'Let's go and bathe, and then I'll start looking for food,' he suggested.

He helped Sue to her feet, and steadied her as she hopped over to the edge of the pool. The ground was already warming up, but it was still bearable under their naked soles. At the edge, Jack stripped off to his underpants, then helped Sue out of her frock. Despite his swim of yesterday, he was still marked and streaked with grime, and there were channels down his skin where the sweat had made itself little river beds through the dust.

Sue's pants, less protected under her frock, were as red as the soil where she had been sitting.

'Come on, Sue. Let's go in in the nude, and we can wash our clothes too.' His jeans and shirt were stiff and itchy from the dried-in dust, and he was sure Sue's were equally uncomfortable.

'We can't. It's rude,' Sue protested.

'Oh don't be silly. It's not rude if there's no one to see us!'

'Well, all right.' Sue supported herself on her good leg, and lifting her bottom managed to wriggle her pants down.

'Ouch!' she complained as she sat back on the bare rock. 'It's scratchy.'

Jack pulled off his pants, too, and dived into the water.

'Now, toss me your things.'

Sue bundled up her clothes, and got ready to throw them.

'No, one at a time. I don't want to drop any, because if I do they'll be gone forever. This pool's pretty deep.'

Piece by piece Jack swished and sloshed each garment around in the water, squeezing and shaking it until he felt it was reasonably clean. Then he spread them carefully around the rocks to dry.

'Okay, now us,' he said, as the last item was laid out and tethered with a stone. He swam back to where Sue was sitting.

'Do you think you can manage it? You can't touch bottom, but if you hang on to the side you'll be all right.'

Gingerly Sue eased herself over the edge. The sunburnt patches stood out, angrily red, against the white of her body. As she lowered herself in, Jack caught a glimpse of her injured foot. It looked swollen and ugly still, and he determined to have a proper look at it as soon as they came out.

'Oooooooh! It's cold!' Sue exclaimed.

'Only at first. Then it's beaut. Swim around a bit to warm up.'

Obediently Sue dog-paddled grimly around in circles, like a small, determined mouse. Jack, meanwhile, had seized a bunch of coarse grass from the edge and was trying to wash himself clean with that. When it proved useless, he grabbed a handful of soil, and scrubbed carefully. As soon as he put his hand in the water, though, the soil filtered out of it. Finally he hoisted himself out on to the bank and gave himself a thorough scrub all over with the gritty soil. When he had finished, he looked like a clay man, with red earth clinging up and down his body.

'Me horrible space monster. Me bunyip from Mars, kill all earth people!' Jack gave a fearsome, Tarzan-like yodel, and leaped back in with a mighty splash that almost swamped Sue. The water made his skin smart and sting where he had rubbed it with the sand. Splashing and diving he washed the last grains off. Finally he surfaced, panting and shaking his head, and flung himself, red and tingling, on to the rocks to dry off. Sue followed his example, but more sedately, and joined him, to lie pleasantly exhausted in the sun.

After a few minutes Jack sat up.

'We don't want to lie here too long, or we'll get sunburned all over.'

He rescued their clothes. They were quite dry, and after

slipping into his own, he helped Sue with hers.

'Now let's have a look at your foot,' he said. 'Is it still sore?'

'Mmm,' Sue considered, 'well, not when I don't move it, it isn't.'

Jack put out his hand, but Sue flinched away before he even touched it. The foot was swollen to almost twice the size of her other one. There was a great, yellowish, semi-circular weal where the drum had landed, while the skin around was mottled blue and green. It was hard to see what was wrong just by looking; the real damage might be inside. Jack wasn't even sure which was dirt and which was damage, for Sue had not been game to try and wash the foot properly. Still, that nasty swelling didn't look too good. Slowly Jack put his hand out again, and touched the bruised area very gently.

'Does that hurt?'

'Yes, but it feels kind of numb, too.'

Jack moved his hand down and tried to flex her toes.

Sue pulled her foot away and lashed out with her other leg, kicking Jack. She caught him off balance, and he sat down with a thump.

'Don't do that. It hurts!'

'I'm only trying to help. I want to find out what's wrong.'

'Well, you're not a doctor, smartypants,' Sue replied crossly.

'Okay. Okay. I didn't mean to hurt you. I'm sorry.'

'Just leave it alone. It'll get better by itself.'

'*Okay,*' repeated Jack, and got stiffly to his feet. It wasn't fair. He was only trying to help. Still, as Sue said, he wouldn't really know anyway, and even if he did, there was nothing he could do about it. He felt pretty sure, though, that her foot must be broken. Or crushed. No, not crushed! Didn't that mean it would go all black, and rot, and have to be cut off? A fellow at school had had his arm crushed by a tractor, and he'd had to have it amputated. But wouldn't Sue's foot have started to go black by now, after all these days if no blood was getting through? It didn't bear thinking about.

'I'm going hunting,' he said gruffly. 'Do you want to go back to the cave?'

Sue shook her head sulkily. She felt guilty for snapping at Jack like that, but he shouldn't have started meddling. Poking around at her foot would only make it worse, not better. It wasn't as though he could *do* anything about it. He was always worrying, even when things couldn't be helped. Still, he had got them here safely. And, despite what he had said, Sue had an inkling that somehow, yesterday, he had saved her life. She mustn't be so mean in future.

'Don't stay in the sun too long, then,' Jack called over his shoulder. He strode over to the cave, picked up the rifle, took a handful of cartridges out of the box, and set off.

As soon as he was out of sight, he sat down and started fiddling with the rifle. He didn't want Sue to know, but he wasn't even sure how to work it. He'd occasionally used a mate's BB rifle, but never a full-sized one. First, he thought, I'll have to see if it's loaded. After a couple of unsuccessful tries he managed to break it open. It was unloaded. He slid a cartridge in, and snapped it shut. Then he snuggled the butt into his shoulder, and squinted at various targets.

Pow! Pow! Pow! Kangaroos, emus, lions, tigers and elephants fell beneath his devastating accuracy. He was the great white hunter whose deadly gun supplied whole safaris with game, while jungle drums beat out a message of menace. Crouched behind a rock; the sun beating down on his scarlet uniform, he held off hordes of turbanned tribesmen in the desolate Khyber Pass. Could he hold them off long enough? Yes, he could hear the bagpipes skirling—reinforcements from the British fort. Flat on his stomach in the dust, he peered between the spokes of a waggon wheel, steadily picking off the circling Redskins who yelled and bit the dust. Behind him crouched the women and children. At last, yelling in fury the Indians withdrew, brandishing their bows and arrows in frustrated rage, for they were unable to succeed against 'Buffalo' Jack Clarke. His keen eye spied a feathered head cautiously peering around a tree. He took aim slowly, and his finger began to press gently on the trigger. Just one shot to prove his marksmanship! He snapped his forefinger quickly in, the gun kicked violently, ramming its butt hard against his shoulder. The noise of the shot started a barrage of scolding from a dozen parrots, who shrieked noisily out of the trees.

Sobered by the sudden racket, Jack ruefully re-loaded the gun, and set his mind to the serious business of hunting.

Where to go was the first problem.

He didn't think there would be much game on the hill itself; it was too steep and bare. From his vantage point, Jack surveyed the plain below him. Not a thing was stirring now as the heat of the day began to envelop the land in its straitjacket of inertia. About half a mile to the north, though, there was a thick clump of trees, that may have marked the meanderings of some long-dead watercourse. Perhaps some animals had holed up there for shade.

Shouldering the re-loaded rifle, and dropping the loose cartridges into his pocket, Jack set off down the hill, and headed in a direct line towards the trees. He hadn't gone far before he realized he should have brought the waterbag with him, for the pulsating heat was almost overpowering. However, he decided it was too far to go back, and the knowledge that there was unlimited water available whenever he chose to return gave him the strength to bear with his thirst for a while.

As he came closer to the scrub, Jack approached more cautiously, taking care to be as silent as possible. His eyes scanned the ground for signs of tracks, but the earth was baked hard and, as far as he could see, he might as well be on the moon.

He wondered if the Aborigines really could track people and animals the way they said. A blade of grass crushed, a pebble disturbed, a twig broken off, a slight scuff mark in the sand were all they relied on. But to Jack the ground looked the same everywhere. There was no grass to crush, and one side of a stone or twig looked the same as any other side as far as he could tell. It was probably all made up. Yet there were stories that were now almost legendary, even a famous one that had happened right in Karkarook itself, about twenty years ago. Little Jamie Bates had wandered off from his parents' caravan, and had been found by old Peter Mulga who had tracked him down over miles and miles of desert. Peter Mulga was now a white-stubbled old man in a flannel shirt and torn dungarees, who never seemed to move from his position on the steps of the Post Office. There he sat all day long, smoking his stubby pipe, and watching with dull eyes the passing traffic. Those eyes could hardly recognize a car from a cart-horse now, and yet it must be true. Jamie Bates still claimed to have dim memories of being picked up and carried home, even though he had only been four at the time. People said that Jamie, or Jim as he now was, regularly gave old Mulga a couple of ounces of tobacco every week. Yes, it seemed true enough, reckoned Jack. But it still seemed impossible, all the same.

While he was puzzling over it, he had drawn steadily nearer and nearer the trees. Now, as he entered their freckled shade, he concentrated entirely on the job he had to do.

Slowly, carefully, he looked around. Then he began to work his way deliberately through the stretch of bush. Relying mainly on what he had seen in films, he picked his way from tree to tree, using whatever bit of cover was available. After every few steps he paused, hoping that if there were an animal about, it would thus not be alarmed. In this way he laboriously covered about half the scrub before he suddenly saw them—two grey kangaroos. They were lying on their sides in the dust, languidly grooming themselves.

Now that the moment had actually come, Jack suddenly felt sick. There were the roos, lying at peace with the world, and he was going to kill them. At the same time, the practical part of his mind told him that it was truly a matter of life or death, not only for the roos, but for him and Sue.

Inch by inch he swung the rifle into position, but the movement, gradual as it was, was enough to alert the two animals. Alarmed, they scrambled to their feet, and the more timid one turned and thudded off through the scrub. The second animal hesitated, its ears pricked forward, forepaws hanging limp and nose twitching, as it sought to scent and assess this strange intruder. Jack sighted along the rifle, shifting his aim to the chest as he decided that the head was too small a target.

As the gun barrel moved the kangaroo, tense, poised for instant fight. In a panic, Jack pulled the trigger. At almost the same second that the gun fired, the roo gave a convulsive leap into the air.

CHAPTER EIGHT

Sue, meanwhile, had moved into the shade of the cave. The first shot, when Jack was involved in his game of make-believe, had startled her with its nearness. For a while she expected Jack to return at any moment with a carcass slung over his shoulder. When he didn't appear, she hopped and hobbled back to the cave, and set about trying to make it into some sort of home.

Her hands throbbed and smarted where the new skin under the raw blisters had contracted tautly, but she managed to organize their few belongings into a neat pile at one end, and then to roll together some stones. These she set in a ring for a fireplace. That would be the kitchen. The waterbag fitted conveniently on to a ledge just above her head.

Next she chose a slightly sloping, sandy patch, and cleared away the stones, twigs and pebbles. Then, using her stick, Sue smoothed the patch as flat as possible, and outlined it with the discarded stones. The bedroom.

Hobbling carefully, and using only the stick, as her arm was still too sore to manage the crutch, she braced herself with her other hand against the rocky wall and went on a brief tour of exploration. At the far end of the cave, the wall jutted out, and round behind this was a small gap in the ground, about a foot wide and several feet deep. There was a rocky ledge on each side of it so you could easily stand astride, and nearby was a mound of rock chips and sandy debris. Sue poked at the mound with the end of her stick and found it was quite soft and crumbly. That, then, could be the lavatory. It was out of sight and more or less private, and the chips and sand could be used to throw in on top of it to stop the flies.

Satisfied with her inspection and her housework, Sue

returned to the main cave and sat down to wait. Sue tried her hand at adding to the Aboriginal drawings on the walls and ceiling, but she couldn't find a suitable stone for drawing. Either they were too soft and fell to pieces when she tried to use them, or so hard that all her pressure only left the faintest mark. Bored, she found a twig and started to play noughts and crosses with herself in the dust. It was then that she heard Jack's second shot from much farther away. She hoped he had shot something, for she was beginning to feel hungry again. She didn't realize that a chop in the butcher's shop is rather different from a meal that has to be skinned, gutted, and dismembered right in front of your eyes.

'Got him!' cried Jack exultantly, as the roo leaped, and he started to run forwards. But the roo had merely swerved in mid-air, and was now crashing off after its fellow. In a frenzy, Jack loaded the gun again, and sent a second shot uselessly after it. Briefly he could hear the sounds of its progress, and then there was silence. Numb with defeat, Jack stood gazing after them.

There was no point in going on now. If there had been any other animals around, the shots and the noise would have scared them all to billy-o. Defeated, thirsty, hungry, and angry, Jack turned and trudged miserably home.

There was no need for Sue to ask him how he had fared. She could see as soon as he climbed into sight that he wasn't carrying any food.

'I don't know,' Jack complained, as he finished telling Sue of his misadventures, 'I had it right in my sights, lined up. I wasn't all that far away, and yet I missed.'

Sue's heart—and her empty stomach—sympathized with Jack.

'How many bullets have you got left?'

'Quite a lot, I think.' Jack dragged a handful from his pocket, while Sue handed over the box of cartridges. He tipped them out, and counted them carefully back.

'Sixty-four.'

'Well, how long would a roo last us?'

'I dunno. The meat would go off pretty quickly in this heat.'

'Yes, but if we cooked it all up at once, and then ate it cold?'

Jack tried to think.

'Well,' continued Sue, 'supposing we had three roos a week. If we were here for two weeks, that'd only be six bullets!'

'I suppose so, but I mightn't hit something every time I shoot. I mightn't ever get *anything*.'

'Well, let's say twelve bullets, or even twenty-four. That still leaves plenty.'

'Plenty for what? What *are* you talking about?'

'For practising!' Sue cried impatiently. 'Why can't you set up a tin or something to aim at?'

'I can shoot all right,' muttered Jack sullenly. The vanished dreams of Jack Clarke, King of the Khyber Rifles, shamed him into a stubborn determination not to admit his shortcomings. 'It's just that this gun kicks so hard it throws my aim off.'

Sue realized her mistake. She had hurt her brother's pride, and boys had such a *thing* about guns and shooting, and being good at that sort of stuff. But she was too annoyed to try to soothe Jack down.

'Well, okay. But even if you are such a flaming good shot, you still need to get used to the rifle.' Jack remained silent.

'Oh, come on!' Sue insisted. 'We've got to eat somehow.'

'Maybe you're right.' Jack got sulkily to his feet. The last thing he wanted to do was to look a fool in front of Sue. It was one thing to play the fool deliberately, to get an audience; it was quite another to be made a fool of against your will.

He grabbed a few cartridges, and one of the morning's empty tins.

'I won't need forty bullets, anyway,' was his parting shot.

He went well out of sight of Sue, and set the tin up on a

rock. Backing away he tried to stand at about the same distance as he had from the kangaroos. The first couple of shots went wide, and Jack realized that he was at a disadvantage aiming at a tin in space, since he hadn't the faintest idea how far he was missing it by. He left the tin, and searched around for a better target. Eventually he found a tree with a large, scarred trunk—an oval patch about a foot long, where the bark was missing. In the centre of this he scratched a rough circle, about three inches in diameter, for the bull's-eye.

Backing off again, he fired several more shots, and then went to examine his marksmanship. Only two of the bullets had even hit the tree, and both of these were well above the bull's-eye. The gun must kick upwards when I fire, he guessed. The next time he aimed lower. The following few rounds were slightly better; at least they were just in the target area even though they were wide of the bull's-eye. Jack also discovered that he seemed to have more control if he squeezed the trigger very gently instead of jerking it quickly as he had been doing. By the time he had used up the last of the bullets, he was feeling considerably happier. Two of his shots had actually nicked the circle, and one had even hit the bull's-eye right inside, even if slightly off centre. And this from a distance of about fifty feet. All he had to do now was to get that close to his prey, and they'd be eating! Shouldering the gun, and swaggering slightly, he returned to Sue.

It was now well into the afternoon, and though Jack wanted to try out his new-found prowess, he didn't think there was much point in returning to where he had found the roos. By now they'd probably be miles away; but tomorrow they'd return, most likely, and then he'd get one. Still, that didn't solve the problem of what to eat tonight.

He wandered over to the pool, and decided he might as well cool off with another swim while he was thinking. He stripped and plunged in, enjoying the water even more now that he was relaxed and rested. Sue hopped over and joined him.

They swam and dog-paddled and duck-dived for a while, then Sue pulled herself out and sat there in her pants while Jack tried doing his 'dead man's float', arms and legs relaxed, body slightly curved, and head hanging down under the water. After doing it several times he ran out of breath and, kicking over, floated on his back.

'We haven't got any food for tonight, have we?' he asked. He had noticed Sue's tidy attempts at housekeeping, even though he had been too cross at the time to comment.

'You saw it, then?' Sue beamed. 'I've got the cave all laid out like a proper house. There's the kitchen, and the bedroom, and the part where we can sit, and there's even a lav.'

'A *lav*? Where?' Jack started to laugh, lost his float-ability, and choked on an unexpected mouthful of water. Threshing and coughing he spluttered to the side and pulled himself out.

'Round the side, down that end.' Sue pointed.

Jack whooped with laughter, rolling around on the rock. At last, gasping, he straightened up and looked at Sue, who was still giggling.

'You really are the end, you know!'

'I am not,' Sue tried to be indignant. 'After all, we've got to go somewhere.'

'We've just got the whole of Australia, practically, that's all,' Jack pointed out.

'You can't just go all over the place,' said Sue primly. 'It brings the flies . . . and . . . and . . . things,' she ended lamely.

'Yes, I suppose so. Anyway, you might put your foot in it—like a cowpat,' hooted Jack. This set them both off in fresh gales of loud laughter, until at last they lay panting and exhausted.

'Still, we haven't solved the problem of what to eat to-night yet,' repeated Jack, when they had finally recovered.

'Can't you try and shoot something else?'

'How can I shoot something *else*, when I haven't shot anything at all?'

'Well, you know what I mean.'

Jack explained why he thought this was a rather futile hope.

'Tomorrow, though,' he promised.

'What about nuts, or berries, or roots, or something?' suggested Sue.

They looked hopefully at the scrub, almost as though they expected it to be miraculously festooned with food. Jack stood up, slipped into his jeans, and went on a short forage.

'There's nothing here,' he reported on his return. 'It'll have to be roots.'

He prowled around, kicking tentatively at different shrubs, and now and again pulling a small plant up and examining it. At last he found one variety that seemed to have thick fleshy roots, rather like a flattened-out bulb. He gathered several of them, brought them over, and washed them in the pool.

He broke a piece off, and sniffed at it doubtfully. It was a brownish-white, and looked like the inside of a rather woody parsnip. He raised it to his mouth.

'What if it's poisonous?' cried Sue suddenly.

'For heaven's sake, Sue, it's not likely. Anyway, it was your idea.'

'But it might be,' insisted Sue, 'lots of berries and plants are poisonous. We did it at school.'

'This isn't a berry, it's a root. And anyway, the Abos live on roots and things.'

'That's waterlily roots.'

'Well, there aren't any waterlilies here, or I would have got them. Just use your eyes.'

'I don't care. What if it was poisonous and you swelled up and died, what would I do?'

Jack wouldn't admit Sue was right, but he was a little bit scared himself now. How did you tell if it was poisonous? He vaguely remembered being told that poisonous plants usually tasted nasty, and that red was Nature's danger signal. Like strawberries? he thought irrelevantly. There was no red on the bush he had pulled up, only grey-green leaves and tiny yellow flowers. Still, he had better be careful all the same.

He broke a very small piece off the root and put it in his mouth. Sue was looking at him as though she expected him to keel over at her feet! He moved the morsel around with his tongue, and then took a careful bite.

'Yurkkkk!' He spat it out, his face twisted with disgust.

'See,' cried Sue triumphantly, 'it was poisoned.'

'Poisoned, my foot. It was just plain awful!'

Jack scooped some water up in his cupped hand and rinsed his mouth out, spitting vigorously.

'It tasted like, well, like burning hot pepper and dirt,' he explained. Sue watched as he grimaced, still trying to scrape the flavour off his taste buds.

'Well, that's out. We'll just have to wait till tomorrow.'

'There is some tea and sugar left,' Sue informed him. 'At least we could have a cup of hot tea.'

'Don't be an idiot. We left the tea and sugar behind, remember?'

'I put them in again.'

'Oh, thanks a lot. As if I didn't have enough to carry already.'

'They didn't weigh that much. And it's a good thing I did, because now it's all we have.'

'Well, I suppose that'd be better than nothing.'

'I've marked out a proper fireplace in the kitchen.'

Jack shrugged on his shirt, Sue wriggled into her dress, and they returned to the cave.

'I'll get some wood.'

Jack set off, and returned soon with an armload of sticks and some dry twigs and leaves to get it going.

Sue had a sudden thought.

'Have we got any matches?'

'Yes, I took a box out of the . . . the car, last thing.'

Jack put his hand into the rear pocket of his jeans, then froze.

'Oh no!' he groaned, and slowly withdrew his hand. In

his palm lay the crushed box. He forced it open and gazed in disbelief at the matches.

'I'd forgotten about them,' he whispered, 'and when I got here yesterday I jumped straight into the pool, clothes and all.' The matches lay stuck together as though still in a sodden heap.

'Wouldn't they have dried out by now?'

'I don't know. I can try.'

Carefully Jack prised the lump apart. A couple of the matches came free, and he knelt down beside the fireplace. But it was no use. As soon as he tried to strike one, the head rubbed off along the box and left the bare matchstick.

'Gosh, I'm sorry, Sue. I completely forgot about them.'

'Oh well, we'll just have to drink water and sugar, cold.'

'I'll spread them out in the sun. Maybe they'll dry out properly.' Jack arranged a little fence of stones, so that there was no chance of any of the matches blowing away, and laid them carefully out.

'I'm not much of a help,' Jack accused himself bitterly. How on earth could he ever have been so stupid, especially after making a point of rescuing the matches from the car?

'Oh yes you are. You got us here, and you saved my life,' defended Sue stoutly. 'We'll be all right after tomorrow.'

'Some hopes! Even if I *do* get us some food, how are we going to cook it?'

'The matches will be dry tomorrow, you'll see,' Sue comforted.

Dinner that night, therefore, turned out to be non-existent. Sue experimented with chewing some tea leaves and sugar together, and declared it was better than nothing. Jack followed her example: it was not unpleasant, but it left his mouth dry and pursed, as though all the saliva had been sucked out. They washed the taste away with copious mugs of water, drinking until their stomachs were blown up—at least they didn't feel quite so hungry that way.

Bloated with water, they drifted into sleep, only to wake up several times during the night to the pangs of hunger. If it's not one thing, concluded Jack sourly, but without much originality, it's another. When we had no water and plenty of food we didn't feel like eating. Now we've got water to drown in, and we look like starving to death!

Early next morning flocks of galahs, wild pigeons and several ducks rowdily shared the waterhole. Jack and Sue, awake early, watched them greedily from the shadow of their overhang. There must be a way to catch some, Jack thought.

'What we want,' Jack told Sue as they discussed the problem after the birds had left, 'is a slingshot or a catapult. But we need some strong rubber and a piece of leather for the stones.'

They looked disconsolately at one another. Sue picked at her thong, but it was too stiff and unyielding to be any good.

'There's elastic in my pants,' she volunteered, with sudden inspiration.

'Hey, that might do!'

Sue wriggled out of the garment in question, and together they investigated it. The elastic was thin and worn, but Jack thought it might just do if several lengths were used on each side. But they still needed the sling. After searching through their few belongings and rejecting each item, it was finally decided to sacrifice Sue's left thong, since she couldn't walk on that foot anyway. The sole was worn fairly thin, and a piece of it, using the two holes through which the straps went, might suffice.

Their work was hampered by the fact that they had omitted to bring a knife with them, and they were reduced to using the blade of the tin opener. After giving Sue detailed instructions, Jack left her to unpick the elastic from her pants and hack the piece of rubber from her thong, while he shouldered the waterbag and rifle and set off again for the patch of scrub where he had fired at the kangaroo yesterday.

He felt giddy from hunger. It was like the other day

when he had drunk the beer, he decided. As well as feeling dizzy if he stood up or stooped quickly, his body had the same remoteness it had had then: as though it didn't quite belong. His hand or his foot would suddenly seem far, far away, or his head would seem incredibly high above the ground. Like Alice in Wonderland, when she grew the snakelike neck, he thought. It was hard to concentrate on what he was doing, and every now and again he felt almost weightless, as though with a good spring he could float up into the air—and stay there.

He wondered if Sue felt the same. They had both had fits of the giggles, over nothing, really; and once or twice Jack thought Sue had looked as if she had been crying. He had felt very close to tears himself from time to time, for no reason at all.

Once again he spent several hours down in the scrub. He quartered it carefully, but saw no sign of life at all, except for the odd crow cawing and wheeling in the sky. Tired out, he squatted down for a drink and a brief rest before starting the long trek home. He raised the waterbag, and was surprised to discover unaccoutable tears mixing saltily with the water. He sat there weakly, his face buried on his knees, unable to stop crying. There were no sobs, just tears flowing silently down his face. At last the tears stopped, of their own accord, and he raised his head limply. Two damp patches stained the knees of his jeans.

He didn't know what to do next.

Part of his mind told him to go on sitting here, forever, if need be. There was no point in trying any more. With an effort, Jack pushed the thought aside, and forced himself to his feet. He picked up the waterbag, and the useless, stupid rifle, and turned towards home.

He trudged back, unseeing, until a slight movement drew his attention. Focusing, Jack saw it was a stumpy-tail lizard waddling slowly along. He let out a hysterical whoop and set off after it. The lizard put on a burst of speed, its body wagging cumbersomely from side to side, but at its fastest it was no quicker than Jack at a slow trot.

Finding its pursuer, almost literally, on its tail, the lizard turned defensively and opened its mouth wide with a ferocious hiss, exposing its bright blue triangular tongue and rosy pink inside cheeks. Jack was undeterred by the lizard's grimace. With a quick movement he put his foot firmly on the lizard's back, pinning it to the ground. Laughing and crying with relief and exultation, he was still careful to pick the lizard up just behind the head. He wasn't sure whether a stumpy-tail's bite was poisonous or not. Most of the boys reckoned all lizard and goanna bites were—if you were bitten, the wound would never heal. Despite his excitement, Jack wasn't going to take any chances!

The lizard was surprisingly strong, and Jack had to drop the waterbag and gun and hold it with both hands. Even then it writhed and squirmed its thick body into half-circles, trying to break free, but the large, shingle-like scales on its back enabled Jack to keep a firm grip. He wasn't quite sure how to carry it home, until he worked out a system by removing one of the leather straps which had been used to fasten the waterbag to the bumper bar of the car. He buckled the strap firmly around the lizard's body. After a few exploratory contortions to try to escape, the reptile hung limply, like a parcel, at the end of its strap.

Proudly bearing his catch, Jack returned to the pool.

During the hours he had been away, Sue had laboriously worked on her thong, gradually hacking out a roughly oval piece from the sole. The edges were jagged and uncertain, but it was usable. Then, after a great deal of struggling and pulling, she had managed to work the straps out of their two holes.

Her eyes widened when she saw Jack's catch.

'How are you going to kill it?'

This was a problem Jack had been avoiding all the way home. It was easy enough to pot something from a distance, but to stand over a captive, even a lizard, and coldly and deliberately kill it, physically, himself, was a task he didn't relish at all. He had already rejected cutting its throat. The skin looked pretty tough and, anyway, they had no knife.

Perhaps he could bash it with a rock? Jack sought around and found a reasonable-sized stone, and hefted it experimentally. But even as he did so, he knew he couldn't use it. At the last minute he would pull his blow, or the lizard would squirm; either way he would make a botch of it. If it couldn't be done in one swift movement, he couldn't do it at all. He saw himself pounding and pounding in a frenzy, trying to kill it, and shuddered. Then his eye fell on the gun.

'I'll shoot it.'

Sue started to smile. It seemed ridiculous to use a *gun* to kill one small lizard. Then she stopped, for she saw the predicament Jack was in; she wouldn't welcome killing it either.

Before his bravado failed, Jack jumped to his feet, lifted the lizard and the rifle, and moved into the open. He dropped the lizard and held it firmly with his foot. Pressing the barrel right against the lizard's head he pulled the trigger. There was a click.

'Oh blast and damn. I forgot to load it.'

Sue, who had her hands over her ears to shut out the bang, her eyes screwed up, and head averted, looked around at the delay.

'Chuck me a bullet, Sue.'

Sue tossed over one from the half empty box, and Jack awkwardly loaded the rifle. He was slightly off balance, with one foot on the lizard trying to hold it still, but not to squash it.

Again Jack aimed the gun, again Sue averted her head. This time the bang shattered the silence, and sent echoes flying around their small enclosure. The lizard twitched as the bullet blasted it into death. As Jack stood back, its body scythed in great arcs from side to side, then it lay still.

Jack picked the corpse up by the strap.

'I'd better skin and gut it,' he said reluctantly. 'Give me the opener.'

'Don't do it right here,' Sue said squeamishly, as she passed over their all-purpose tool. 'Take it over into the bush so there won't be any mess.'

Jack moved off unwillingly to his distasteful task. The tin opener proved a barely effective knife, and he found the job even messier and more unpleasant than he had feared. The small, blunt blade made little impression on the scaly skin, and it took some time before he managed to get the belly open. Once gutted, and with the skin inexpertly peeled off, the rather mangled flesh seemed a wretched offering indeed. Returning via the pool, Jack dunked the carcass in the water to clean it, and scrubbed his messy hands.

He left the dripping body with Sue, and went off to try the matches. Here he had no luck at all. The solid soaking they had received had ruined them for good. Jack made a couple of futile attempts to get one to light, but each match gave, at the most, a fizzly flare that sputtered out before a proper flame could burn. In desperation, Jack bunched the remaining six or eight together, and tried lighting them all at once. It was the last chance. Holding them close to the pile of dry leaves, Jack struck them quickly. A brief flame flared from one to another. Before it could go out, Jack dropped the lot on to the leaves and blew cautiously. A few sparks caught and burned little rapid half-circles out of the top leaves. Jack dropped on a scattering of dried grass and continued to blow with feverish tension. A wisp of blue smoke spiralled up from the centre, and suddenly the whole pile burst into flames. Quickly Jack added twigs, then sticks, until he was sure that the fire was feeding properly.

'It's going, Sue—the fire's going!' he yelled jubilantly.

Sue hopped over as Jack did a sort of war-dance around the blaze.

'We'll have to make sure it doesn't go out again, because that's the end of the matches.'

'That'll be my job, then,' Sue offered, glad to have some responsibility. She found sitting all day, while Jack was out looking for food, terribly dull.

'Yes. I'll lay in a supply of wood, and you can be "Guardian of the Sacred Flame". It won't need to be a big blaze all the time, as long as it stays alight.'

Feeling carefree and happy for the first time, Jack bounded over to the nearest bush, and stripped off some long, thin, greenish twigs. The lizard was chopped into joints, roughly skewered on the sticks, and roasted. The result was more burnt than cooked, and almost tasteless without salt, but already they felt better. At Sue's suggestion, they boiled the billy, and sparingly made some tea. The lizard had only taken the sharp edge off their hunger, but after they had eaten and drunk they both felt inanely cheerful.

This was only the beginning. Now they had a fire and had managed to find their first lot of food, the future seemed almost rosy.

Jack spent the rest of the afternoon constructing his shanghai. It took a lot of fiddling, and even then he wasn't particularly satisfied with the result. The elastic had very little force to it. Sue's pants, like all their clothes, were worn until the last bit of water had been wrung out of them.

When the catapult was finished, Jack collected a supply of suitably sturdy pebbles, and had some practice shots. The sling threw the pebbles with reasonable accuracy, but not much power or distance. With a bit of extra luck, Jack hoped, a direct hit might stun or disable a bird temporarily, so that he could run in and grab it before it recovered. But he reckoned it would have to be a particularly well-aimed, or lucky, shot to the head to be much good.

He had a chance to try it later that day when he spotted a small flock of galahs feeding on the ground. Jack approached as close as he dared. The one nearest to him seemed to be sick. He didn't relish the idea of eating a sick bird, but then he decided to settle for what he could get. Maybe it was just old anyway. Trying to look as inconspicuous and as much like a tree as possible, he edged nearer. The birds had stopped feeding and were now eyeing him warily. Each time Jack took a step, the whole flock also moved forward, so that they kept the same relative distance from him.

He sidled a bit closer, and stopped. One or two of the more nervous birds took to the air and flapped off, circling to rest in a fringe of scrub. Another two steps, and the whole group broke, winging off with discordant shrieks of warning. Only the sick bird remained. More confidently, Jack walked towards it, and it turned and ran with an awkward, stumbling, flat-footed lumber. Jack quickened his pace. He was certain, now, that the bird was unable to fly for some reason or another, and he wanted to get close enough for a really effective shot. The galah still stumbled ahead of him, and Jack broke into a sprint. Perhaps he could even run it down.

By now the flock had reached the safety of the scrub, from whence they called advice and encouragement to their fellow. As if this was a signal, the ailing bird suddenly spread its wings and took off easily and effortlessly to join the others. Jack realized he had been fooled by a simple decoy act: the one galah had stayed there, distracting his attention until the rest of the flock was safe. It was no sicker than Jack was, and certainly not as hungry. Angrily Jack chucked a pebble after the pink and grey feathers, and swore disgustedly.

He followed the birds over to the scrub, at which point they took off jeeringly for safer quarters; but by now Jack was not so concerned with them as with the possibility of finding eggs.

It was hard to tell which might be a nest, and which was just untidy scrub, for many bunches of twigs could just as easily be a tatty, slipshod nest or a natural growth. An hour's searching and a number of tricky climbs resulted in numerous scratches and five eggs, all small. Jack only hoped they were not too ripe as he carefully carried them back to Sue.

On the way he saw a small goanna. He piled the eggs on the ground and tried to catch it. At first the goanna froze into immobility, but as it saw that the enemy continued to approach, it turned and took off with a jolt that raised an explosion of red dust where it had been standing. Jack chased it for a few yards, but the goanna put on a burst of speed that easily outpaced its pursuer, its legs pedalling furiously, its body weaving rapidly from side to side, snake-like, as it darted away. It was futile to continue, and Jack quickly gave up. The goanna ran a few more yards, then veered sideways to a halt, safely out of range. It regarded Jack out of one mocking reptilian eye, occasionally flicking its tongue in and out to taste the likelihood of further danger.

Jack kicked angrily at odd stones as he made his way back to the eggs. It seemed as though every bird and animal was conspiring to make a fool of him. For a few moments of panic, Jack couldn't even find the eggs, for they had merged in with the sandy background. It was only when he spotted his slingshot lying in the dirt that he was able to pinpoint them.

Hardboiled eggs, a bare mouthful in each, and sweet black tea made a barely adequate evening meal. The eggs had been strong and pongy, but whether this was because they were rather elderly, or merely their natural flavour, they couldn't decide.

Yet, lying there idly, the flames flickering, Jack felt strangely secure. It was all up to him, and if he failed, then they would both be lost. But he wouldn't fail. Today had been only the start: with one lizard and five eggs his luck had changed. There *was* enough food about to keep them alive—just—even if they had to live mainly on lizards and suchlike.

Sue rolled over on to her back and stared at the first stars, gleaming palely in the green-tinged sky.

'What if the fire goes out during the night?'

Jack frowned. The fire was now his main worry. The wood, old and dry, and much of it half rotten, burned away with frightening speed, and left ashes rather than coals.

'I dunno,' he offered unhelpfully. 'I should've got a really thick log that would've kept going all night.'

'Where from?' Sue looked around at the thin and straggly bush, just visible in the gathering dusk.

'Down below, where I've been hunting. There's a lot of big stuff around down there, and I could probably cart some up.'

'Sooner you than me,' observed Sue.

They fell silent for a while. Jack pulled a gum leaf off a branch, and tried blowing it. All that resulted were a few 'raspberries'. Sue giggled.

'Give us a go,' she demanded, stretching out her hand.

'This one's mine. You have your own.' Jack stripped off a handful and passed them across to Sue.

They sucked and blew explosively for a few minutes, then Sue managed to produce an unearthly, off-key screech from hers. She tried again but, fortunately for their ear drums, was unsuccessful.

'It makes my lips all tickly,' she complained, dropping the leaf into the fire.

'Don't do that!' exclaimed Jack in pretended horror. 'You have to go on practising. Then when we get home we can earn pots of money as a gum leaf band.'

'You are a nit!' Sue laughed.

Jack sprang to his feet and, holding his nose, made a series of high-pitched whining noises as he marched up and down. He finished with an elaborate flourish.

'There. Wouldn't you pay quids for a performance like that?' he asked.

'Only if I was off my head, and deaf as well,' replied Sue, with sisterly candour.

'Some people have no soul,' Jack complained as he settled down by the fire again. 'I reckon,' he continued, when he had recovered his breath, 'we'd better take it in turns watching the fire tonight.'

'Okay. Who'll take first turn? I will.' Sue answered her own question before Jack had time to speak. 'I'm not tired.'

'Me neither.'

'You should be, you've done all the work today.'

'Yes, well . . .' Jack gave in. He wasn't actually tired, only rather listless, but he'd found that any prolonged activity quickly used up his small reserve of energy.

Sue interrupted his reveries.

'How long will we have for each turn? We haven't any way of keeping time.'

'That's a thought. I suppose we'd each better go as long as we can, and then wake the other.'

'Fair enough,' agreed Sue.

Until quite late they chatted in fits and starts and long silences, with the relaxed companionship that a campfire, no matter where, brings. But, inevitably, the conversation turned again and again to food.

'I can get grass seeds,' Sue promised. Pounded up between two stones and mixed with water, they might not be very appetizing, but at least they would provide a bit of extra bulk.

They tried to remember what they had learned in Social Studies about the Aborigines and other hunting peoples. Jack was concentrating on the ducks which still visited the waterhole. Perhaps there was some way of sneaking up on them while they were swimming and catching them by the legs.

'It would be better than trying to shoot them,' he explained to Sue, for he doubted if he could hit so small a target. He certainly couldn't hope to bring one down in flight. He also determined to climb up to the higher level tomorrow and see what was there.

'A snare or a trap would be good for catching birds. Like that one I had at home, remember?'

Jack had used an old box propped up by a twig. The twig could be pulled away by a piece of string once the bird had entered. In this way he had caught several parrots and cockatoos which he had sold around the town for a bit of extra money. The only drawback was that they didn't have a box or a length of string. They might be able to make a string by knotting some of the tough grasses together, but the box was a different matter. The only receptacle of any sort was the billy, and that was too small. Also, they didn't have any wheat to use as bait. Regretfully, the idea was discarded.

Sue was keen on the possibility of making a snare of some sort.

'Lots of birds come here during the day,' she pointed out. 'If I made a sort of noose, with a running knot, a bird might just tread in it, and then I could jerk the noose tight, and catch it by the leg.'

Jack was going to tell Sue that even if it worked, grass would hardly be strong enough to hold a bird, but he decided not to.

'Well, I suppose it's worth a try,' he conceded. Sue was alone for much of the day, and it would give her something to do. Also, there was just the chance that it might work, though he didn't think it very likely. Anything that might, even remotely, add to their larder should be considered.

Gradually Jack drifted off into a doze, through which he was vaguely conscious of Sue moving every now and again to replenish the fire. He must have gone right off eventually, for he woke with a start to find Sue shaking him. Jack stretched and sat up to take over his watch, while Sue curled into sleep beside him.

It was hard to stay awake in the middle of the night. Jack tried to estimate the time by watching the stars as they changed position, but they moved too slowly. Besides, as he didn't know which particular star he was looking at, nor how long it took to move, he wasn't much farther ahead.

His head began to nod, so he tried to concentrate fiercely on food. A dozen meat pies, their lids flaked back, and islets of spicy-sweet tomato juice floating redly on the meat and gravy. He imagined biting through the crispy pastry into the squishy centre, carefully manœuvring so that none of the juice squeegeed out; licking the drops that threatened to fall; sucking out the succulent filling before each bite. Or fish and chips would be good, all rolled up in white butcher's paper, with an outer layer of newspaper. He'd tear off the top of the cylindrical package, peel off a bit of batter, pick out a hot salty chip, pull off the white fishy flakes, and lick his greasy fingers to cool them down as they became too hot and burning in his eagerness. Then he'd have a great frothing milkshake: chocolate with malt and double ice cream. There would be little beads of moisture on the metal holder it was mixed in. He'd use two straws, and the thick sweet creamy liquid would coat his mouth and tongue, and he'd suck and suck until the last sudden gurgle of emptiness—and then order another. Or maybe a plate of sausages with onion gravy and a couple of fried eggs, and thick slabs of bread and butter and jam. That really sticks to a fellow's insides. Jack could taste it all so intensely that for a moment he even imagined that the fire crackling was the sizzling of sausages, and the whiff of wood smoke was the savoury tang of cooking food.

Shaking his head, he brought himself back to the reality of the present: to an empty rumbling stomach, and the promise of food only if he was skilful enough to find any.

A pale lemon tinge to the sky promised that dawn would soon be coming. Jack was unbearably drowsy, but it seemed a shame to wake Sue again for such a short time. Daylight, and the birds' chorus, would rouse them soon enough. Carefully he built up the fire, adding a few chunks of solid-looking wood which, he estimated, would burn until well after the sun was up, and fell asleep.

It was full sunlight when he awoke with a start. He sat up guiltily to check on the fire. With a sigh of relief he saw that Sue was already up and the fire was still burning low but well.

'A fat lot of good you are,' she jeered. 'I woke up to find you snoring your head off, and the fire left to look after itself.'

'Okay, okay, don't rouse on me.' Jack pretended to cower away from her reproaches. 'It was nearly light when I went to sleep, and I built the fire up so it'd last before turning in. It seemed silly to wake you when the night was just about over.'

'That's what you say,' kidded Sue. 'You probably spent the whole night asleep.'

'Oh, don't be silly,' Jack replied, slightly shamefaced. After all, what if he had guessed wrong, and the fire had gone out? It would have been his fault, and they really would have been in a mess.

CHAPTER NINE

It was now, perhaps, the eleventh day. Sue had scratched a rough calendar of the time since they had first set out from Karkarook. They were both a bit confused about the early period, when the days still seemed jumbled up, and Sue admitted that her calendar was only partly accurate. Looking at the strokes scratched on the rock wall of their cave, Sue hoped, for the thousandth time, that someone would start looking for them soon. Mostly she believed that someone would, but occasionally she lost heart. Supposing it was just thought that Uncle Bert had made a good strike and was staying on? Then they wouldn't be missed until the school holidays were over. That would be at least another two weeks—and every day they were growing a little weaker.

All the tea and sugar had long since given out, and snakes, small lizards, and stumpy-tails were now their main fare. These were boiled up in the billy, but they were pretty unappetizing without any seasoning. Sue collected all the grass seeds that she could, and pounded them up to add to their stews, but that only gave them a few extra mouthfuls each day. She had also experimented cautiously with roots and leaves and berries, but she hadn't found anything in sufficient quantities to make much difference to their diet. Moreover, twice they had suffered from severe stomach cramps, and after the second time, they had both agreed not to try any more new plants. It was difficult enough to manage on what they *were* eating, without running the risk of losing a meal.

Jack, too, was worried. He had had a few more shots at kangaroos, but without success, and he carried the rifle now mainly for moral support..Despite his care, the supply of cartridges was running low, and he was forced to overcome his squeamishness and kill any game he caught with a large rock. He had explored the upper pool: nothing new there. On the way up he had seen a fat arrowhead imprint in some soft sand, and that meant there were emus about, but they never saw any. Once he did find a solitary emu egg, but when he broke it open it proved to be addled, and the stench made him sick.

So much of their time was spent in stalking, searching, waiting. Sue could now just hobble around on her injured foot, but she still could not go far from the camp. The adventure and excitement of playing Swiss Family Robinson, which had helped to sustain them at first, had gradually vanished, and time expanded into an empty boring vacuum. So, in the heat of the day they usually played whatever games they could adapt to the wilderness: Boxes, and Noughts and Crosses drawn in the sand, I Spy, tossing pebbles into the billy, and word games. Sue usually won these last, for she was a much better speller than Jack.

She dragged her thoughts back from the past as Jack gave in once again.

'C-I-N-N-A M-O-N,' she crowed triumphantly.

'That's not right,' complained Jack. 'There's only one "n", and it begins with an "s".'

'It does not!'

'It does too!'

'You can't spell for sour apples. You never could.'

'I mightn't be able to spell, but I don't cheat, either.'

'I'm not cheating,' Sue flared.

'You are. Cheat, *cheat*, CHEAT!'

'Shut UP!' Sue grabbed a handful of sand and flung it at Jack. 'Spoilsport. I hate you!'

Jack scrambled to his feet, half blinded. He was choking with a rage he had never felt before. He made a move towards Sue, and raised his foot as if to kick her.

'Don't you dare!' she yelled, grabbing another handful of sand.

Jack glared at her, rubbing his stinging eyes.

'You . . . you . . . bloody bitch!' he spat. 'You can starve to death for all I care!'

He turned and stamped off, making his way up to the higher pool. Once there he sat on the edge, dangling his feet in the water, then after a while he stripped off and dived in. He stayed away for the rest of the afternoon, swimming and sunbaking with feigned indifference. His anger had evaporated rapidly, to be replaced by a sullen resentment. He was damned if he'd go back: see how she liked *that*!

As evening approached, the ducks came whirring over, and saw with dismay that their new refuge was invaded. Jack watched them come, and realized it was late. He was sick of swimming by himself, and he had been in the water so long that the skin on his hands was wrinkled and crêpy. He climbed out of the pool and dressed. What if Sue had been mad enough to let the fire go out? Besides there was still some stewed snake left over from breakfast, and he was ravenous.

He went back.

Sue was making a great business of tending the stew.

'Where've *you* been?' she demanded.

'Up in the pool.' Jack felt his temper rising again at her aggressive tone.

'I thought at least you'd have got some more food.' Sue looked at him, and her eyes were red.

'I'm sorry,' she added, and burst into sobs. 'I didn't mean to be cranky, but I was afraid you really had gone off and left me.'

'Don't be silly,' he said uncomfortably.

'No. It was all my fault, and I really am sorry.'

'Oh, for heaven's sake!' Jack was embarrassed. 'You'll drown the stew if you're not careful.'

Sue sniffed, then giggled.

'It could do with some salt.' She wiped her eyes. 'Here, I'll dish it up.'

Jack sat down beside her, and gave her a quick hug.

To his surprise, he found that their sudden quarrel, instead of creating a barrier between them, seemed to have brought them closer together as if, by showing themselves at their worst, they now had nothing more to hide. In the past they had talked about food, and the practicalities of surviving. This night they gradually turned to the past, and talked about Karkarook; in the end, almost shyly, they began to talk about themselves.

'I wish Mum was still alive,' Sue said quietly, after a particularly long pause.

Jack was startled.

'I didn't think you even remembered her. You were only six when she died.'

'Five,' Sue corrected. 'I don't suppose I do really remember her properly. Not what she looked like and all that, but just as a sort of . . . well . . . person. Whenever I try to remember her face, though, I get all mixed up with the others.'

By 'the others' Jack knew Sue mean the succession of 'mums' their father had brought home after their mother had died. None of them had stayed very long, and most of them drank. The ones who didn't drink were worse than the ones who did, for they were always arguing and quarrelling with Dad over money. Jack could recall a few of them quite clearly, but the rest blurred into a composite picture.

Sue's voice broke into his thoughts.

'I wonder what happened to Hazel?'

Hazel had been Sue's favourite, Jack's too. She had learned cooking and sewing from the nuns at an Aboriginal Mission, and she had been the only one who had looked after them properly.

'I don't know. There was a whole lot of trouble down at the Blacks' Camp—you know, fights and drinking and all that.' Jack strained to remember. 'They brought bulldozers in and knocked the camp down, so all the Abos left. Hazel, too, I suppose. She once said she had a blackfellow husband as well. Perhaps she liked him better than Dad.'

'I cried for days after she left,' Sue admitted.

'I know. *And* Dad went on a colossal binge.'

'I wonder why there weren't any more after Hazel?'

'Maybe Dad was afraid of getting stuck with another Betty,' said Jack ruefully.

'She was horrible,' Sue shuddered.

Jack agreed. Betty had been by far the worst. She had had a terrible temper, and used to whale into them with sticks of kindling wood. She'd whale into Dad, too, given half a chance. Even now Jack could see his father, arms flung up in front of his face, mumbling, 'Don' . . . don' hit me, love,' while Betty set on to him with whatever was handy.

They were both silent for a long time, looking inward.

'You know,' said Sue at last, 'Dad must have been awfully lonely and unhappy to put up with people like Betty.'

Jack hesitated. His father was . . . his father. He'd never thought about him having feelings before; he was just someone who was there, ready-made, as it were, who did certain things and reacted in certain ways. When Mum had died, Jack had been lonely and unhappy, and he knew Sue had been, too. But he had been too young to put himself in his father's place and realize that adults, also, could suffer. It certainly hadn't occurred to him since.

Lonely?

'Yes, I suppose he was,' he answered thoughtfully. 'Mum was awfully nice, and she never got really cranky with Dad. Of course, he didn't drink nearly as much then, either.'

'What was she like?'

'Who? Mum?'

Sue nodded.

'Well, you've seen her picture.' There was a sepia wedding photo on the wall of the bedroom. It showed a young woman, her hair swept unfashionably high on top of her head, smiling rigidly at the camera. But even when Mum had been alive, this photo had seemed to have no connection with his mother. Jack tried to explain it further, but his memories were vague.

'She was skinny, like you, and . . . well . . . nice. And a beaut cook. I think she was a school teacher before she married Dad.'

'That's funny. I want to be a teacher, too.'

For the second time that night Jack was startled. He'd never given his own future much thought, and here was Sue with hers all planned.

'Why, for heaven's sake?'

'Well, I like school,' said Sue defensively, 'and I'm good at lessons. I just think it'd be nice to teach other kids. Little kids, you know, in primary school, not big kids. I'd have to win a scholarship, though, and go to the city to study. Then I could get a job anywhere, in all different towns.'

'You've really got it all figured out,' Jack said with admiration. His own aims were not nearly so clear cut.

Mainly he wanted to leave school as soon as possible and get a job. His local heroes were the shearers, station hands and drovers who periodically appeared in Karkarook to go on a spree. With their brightly checked shirts, dusty boots and sunburned swagger, their easy assurance, and adult talk of sheep, and roos, and girls, and booze, they had seemed to him the ultimate in masculine sophistication.

Now he had time to think past their superficial appeal, past the present. For many of them it was an aimless existence, with no real security; they ended their days sitting in the sun outside some pub, hands hanging idly across their knees, and eyes gazing into nothingness. Jack saw that future with sudden clarity, and rejected it. There were exceptions, of course, if you were a top-notch drover, or a 'gun' shearer, or . . . Uncle Bert. He'd had a happy life—and he had no future to worry about now, either.

He became aware of Sue looking at him impatiently.

'Wake up, stupid, I asked you a question.'

'Sorry, I was daydreaming.'

'I said, what do *you* want to be?'

'I was just thinking about it.'

'You'll have to decide pretty soon. You haven't got much longer before you finish school.'

'Oh, don't be such a Miss Bossy Boots.' Jack poked irritably at the fire.

'You used to say you wanted to be a soldier,' persisted Sue.

'That's when I was younger.'

'Like last month? You definitely said, just before Christmas . . .'

'Well, I've changed my mind,' Jack interrupted firmly.

It was true, though. He had wanted to join the Army: it was so easy and simple—just obey orders, and you couldn't go wrong. Now he wasn't so sure. In a strange sort of way he had actually *enjoyed* the responsibilities of the past two weeks, even though there had been cold terror at the pit of his stomach, for then had come the warm glow of achievement: getting the fire going, catching his first food, *keeping them both alive all that time.*

No, there must be something else. He wasn't sure what, but with time he knew he could find something better. He might even learn a trade—just so long as it wasn't a dead end. From now on he was going to be his own boss.

Next morning, as if to prove his new-found confidence, he managed, by a lucky fluke, to wing a duck. It panicked into the air, flew unsteadily for a moment or two, then crashed into the scrub. After a brief but anxious search, Jack retrieved the wounded bird and strutted back to camp. There had been nothing for breakfast, so they cooked it at once and filled themselves up with the tough, gamey flesh. This latest success sent their spirits sky-high. Perhaps it was this triumph, too, that gave them the confidence to approach the one subject they had both avoided: the subject they had, as though by mutual agreement, never discussed between themselves.

Again it was Sue who made the opening move. She wasn't sure what Jack's reaction would be, so she strove to keep her voice as casual as possible.

'I wonder how Dad's going,' she asked, almost to herself. 'He's never been alone before.'

'You mean the town drunk?' Jack hopped up and began his famous imitation, then stopped, frozen and ashamed. His face reddened beneath his mahogany tan.

'I didn't mean that, Sue.' With eyes averted, he scuffed the ground with his toe. 'I . . . I guess he's going all right.

Anyway, we'll be back soon to look after him.' He heard his own words with amazement, yet he knew they were true.

Suddenly he understood that he and Sue were the strong ones: they would go on surviving, no matter how long it took. He thought back over their trek to the hills, the awful struggle to carry Sue up to the pool, and the endless hunt for food. *They* had fought the odds and survived—it was Dad who was weak and sick and defeated. He and Dad had both had to battle and fight, but he had won and Dad had lost. His own battles weren't over, yet, Jack knew. He would have to go on fighting—and winning—because he'd still hate to see Dad drunk, and he'd still be hurt by other people's gibes and laughter.

But that was only on the surface; and the surface wasn't important any more.

Then, crazily, out of the blue, Sue was shaking and pummelling him.

'Listen! Listen!' she screamed.

'How can I listen when you're making all that row!'

Sue subsided, and Jack became aware of a distant, angry buzzing.

A swarm of bees?

It was a *plane*!

He spun round and scanned the sky. Far to the east a silver dot inched towards them.

'There it is, I see it!' yelled Sue. 'It's a search plane. They're looking for us!'

'Quick, build up the fire!'

Sue threw the remaining wood on to the flames, knocking the billy over in her excitement.

'Smoke!' cried Jack. He darted out and tore furiously at the nearest bushes, stripping off handfuls of leaves. He ran back and flung them at Sue, then raced off for more. Sue piled them on top of the fire, then more and more, as Jack kept running back with fresh supplies.

The thrumming of the engine was loud now. With agonizing slowness, tiny curls of smoke tendrilled up through the heap of green leaves.

'Hall-oo-o-o-o!' Jack leaped wildly about, waving his arms and yelling like a madman, although he knew the pilot couldn't possible hear him. He ripped his shirt off and began to wave it frantically—then suddenly he stopped.

'It's no use,' he said. 'It's going too far north to see us. It can't have been looking for us after all; it must be a private plane.'

He flung his shirt down bitterly.

Sue stared at the column of smoke now rising thickly from the fire, then raised her eyes to the gradually diminishing plane.

'Jack!' She dug her fingers into his arm. Almost disbelievingly she whispered, 'It's turning.'

He looked up. The plane swung round in a lazy arc, and headed back towards them.

'Your shirt. Wave your shirt!' cried Sue.

Jack picked it up and waved it steadily from side to side. He was no longer leaping about, but a great grin had spread across his face. The plane came nearer and nearer, and then was directly overhead. They could see two faces peering down from the cockpit windows. The plane circled again and came back. As it neared them this time, the pilot dipped the wings to show he had seen their signal. It passed low overhead, and Jack saw one of the occupants give the 'thumbs up' sign for good luck. Once more the plane circled, then turned away, and headed towards the east—the way it had come.

They watched until it disappeared over the horizon, and then they watched the sky until the last faint drone had died away.

'They're going back to get help. Come on, Sue, let's have a swim to celebrate!'

The Shape of Three

LILITH NORMAN

'Hey!' Greg shouted as some one crashed into him from behind at the crowded showground. He turned round angrily to insult the cause of the accident, but instead his mouth fell open with amazement. There, standing in front of him, Greg saw the mirror image of himself . . .

From the moment they met, Greg and his double Bruce felt the special bond that linked them. But having a double proved not to be the fun they had hoped; instead it threw their vastly different families into fear and confusion. Besides, Greg's real twin brother, who was as different from him as day from night, felt a jealous hatred for Bruce. And then finally came the awful discovery that changed their lives.

A gripping story for readers of ten and up.